WAITING
on
GOD

Register This New Book

Benefits of Registering*

- ✓ FREE **replacements** of lost or damaged books
- ✓ FREE **audiobook** – *Pilgrim's Progress*, audiobook edition
- ✓ FREE information about new titles and other **freebies**

www.anekopress.com/new-book-registration

*See our website for requirements and limitations.

WAITING
on
GOD

A 31-Day Study

ANDREW MURRAY

ANEKO PRESS

We love hearing from our readers. Please contact us at www.anekopress.com/questions-comments with any questions, comments, or suggestions.

Waiting on God – Andrew Murray

Revisions Copyright © 2018

Originally published by Fleming H. Revell Company; New York | Chicago | Toronto

Unless otherwise noted, scripture quotations are taken from the Jubilee Bible, copyright © 2000, 2001, 2010, 2013 by Life Sentence Publishing, Inc. Used by permission of Life Sentence Publishing, Inc., Abbotsford, Wisconsin. All rights reserved.

Scripture quotations marked (RSV) are from Revised Standard Version of the Bible, copyright © 1946, 1952, and 1971 National Council of the Churches of Christ in the United States of America. Used by permission. All rights reserved.

Cover Design: Natalia Hawthorne

Cover Photography: EastVillage Images/Shutterstock

eBook Icon: Icons Vector/Shutterstock

Editors: Sheila Wilkinson and Ruth Zetek

Aneko Press

www.anekopress.com

Aneko Press, Life Sentence Publishing, and our logos are trademarks of

Life Sentence Publishing, Inc.
203 E. Birch Street
P.O. Box 652
Abbotsford, WI 54405

RELIGION / Christian Life / Spiritual Growth

Paperback ISBN: 978-1-62245-543-0

eBook ISBN: 978-1-62245-544-7

10   9   8   7   6   5   4   3   2

Available where books are sold

Contents

Wait Thou Only upon God

My soul, wait thou only upon God.
– Psalm 62:5 KJV

*A God . . . which worketh for him that waiteth
for Him.* – Isaiah 64:4

Wait only upon God; my soul, be still,
    And let thy God unfold His perfect will,
Thou fain wouldst follow Him throughout this year,
Thou fain with listening heart His voice wouldst hear,
Thou fain wouldst be a passive instrument
Possessed by God, and ever Spirit-sent
Upon His service sweet – then be thou still,
For only thus can He in thee fulfill
His heart's desire. Oh, hinder not His hand,
From fashioning the vessel He hath planned.

Be silent unto God, and thou shall know
The quiet, holy calm He doth bestow
On those who wait on Him; so shalt thou bear
His presence, and His life and light e'en where

The night is darkest, and thine earthly days
Shall show His love, and sound His glorious praise.
And He will work with hand unfettered, free
His high and holy purposes through thee.

First *on* thee must that hand of power be turned,
Till in His love's strong fire thy dross is burned,
And thou come forth a vessel for thy Lord,
So frail and empty, yet, since He hath poured
Into thine emptiness His life, His love,
Henceforth through thee the power of God shall move
And He will work *for* thee. Stand still and see
The victories thy God will gain for thee;
So silent, yet so irresistible,
Thy God shall do the thing impossible.

Oh, question not henceforth what thou canst do;
Thou canst do *nought.* But He will carry through
The work where human energy had failed,
Where all thy best endeavours had availed
Thee nothing. Then, my soul, wait and be still;
Thy God shall work for thee His perfect will.
If thou wilt take no less, *His best* shall be
Thy portion now and through eternity.

> – Freda Hanbury

Excerpt from Address in Exeter Hall

May 31, 1895

I have been surprised at nothing more than the letters that have come to me from missionaries and others from all parts of the world. These devoted men and women testify to the need they feel in their work of a deeper and a clearer insight into all that Christ could be to them. Let us look to God to reveal Himself among His people in a measure very few have realized. Let us expect great things of our God.

Too little time is given to waiting on God at our conventions and assemblies. Isn't He willing to make things right in His own divine way? Has the life of God's people reached the utmost limit of what God is willing to do for them? Surely not. We want to wait on Him and put away our experiences, however blessed they have been; our concept of truth, however sound and scriptural we think it is; our plans, however needful and suitable they appear. We want to give God time and place to show us what He could do and what He will do. God has new developments and new resources. He can do new things, unheard-of things, and hidden things. Let us enlarge our hearts and not limit Him. *As thou didst come down when thou didst terrible things we did not look for, that the mountains flowed down at Thy presence* (Isaiah 64:3).

Andrew Murray

Preface

Previous to leaving home for England last year, I had been impressed by the thought of how, in all our religion, personal and public, we need more of God. I had felt that we needed to train our people in their worship to wait on God and make the cultivation of a deeper sense of His presence, more direct contact with Him, and entire dependence on Him a more definite aim of our ministry. At a welcome breakfast in Exeter Hall, I expressed this thought in connection with all our religious work. I have already said that I was surprised at the response to this opinion. I saw that God's Spirit had been working the same desire in many hearts.

The experiences of the past year, both personal and public, have greatly deepened my conviction. It is as if I am only beginning to see the deepest truth confirming God and our relationship to Him center in this waiting on God. I see how very little in our life and work we have been surrounded by its spirit. The following pages are the outcome of my conviction and the desire to direct the attention of all God's people to the one great remedy for all our needs. More than half of these pieces were written on board ship; I fear they bear the marks of being somewhat crude and hasty. In looking them over, I have felt that I should write them over again. But this I cannot now do, so I send them out with the prayer that He who loves to use the feeble may give His blessing with them.

I do not know if it will be possible for me to put into a few words what are the chief things we need to learn. In a note about William Law at the close of this book, I have mentioned some. But what I want to say here is this: the great lack of our religion is that *we do not know God.* The answer to every complaint of feebleness and failure, the message to every congregation or convention seeking instruction on holiness, ought to be simply, "What is the matter: Do you not have God?" If you really believe in God, He will make all things right. God is willing and able by His Holy Spirit. Cease from expecting the least good from yourself or the least help from anything that is in man and just yield yourself unreservedly to God to work in you; He will do all for you.

How simple this looks! And yet we know so little of this gospel. I feel ashamed as I send these defective meditations; I can only cast them on the love of my brethren and of our God. May He use them to draw us all to Himself and to learn in practice and experience the blessed art of *waiting only upon God.* If only we could get the right perception of what the influence would be on a life spent not in thought or imagination or effort but in the power of the Holy Spirit, wholly waiting upon God.

With my greeting in Christ to all God's saints that it has been my privilege to meet, and to those I have not met, I subscribe myself as your brother and servant,

Andrew Murray

Wellington, 3 March 1896

The God of Our Salvation

Truly my soul waiteth upon God: from him cometh my salvation. – Psalm 62:1 KJV

If salvation indeed comes from God and is entirely His work, as our creation was, it follows that our first and highest duty is to wait on Him to do the work that pleases Him. Waiting becomes the only way to fully experience salvation, the only way to know God as the God of our salvation. All the difficulties that keep us back from completely experiencing salvation have their cause in this one thing: the defective knowledge and practice of waiting upon God.

All that the church and its members need for the manifestation of the mighty power of God in the world is the return to our true place, the place that belongs to us in both creation and redemption, the place of absolute and unceasing dependence upon God. Let us strive to see what the elements are that make up this most blessed and needful waiting upon God. It may help us to discover the reasons why this grace is so neglected and to feel how infinitely desirable it is that the church, that we ourselves, should at any price learn the blessed secret of waiting.

The deep need for this waiting on God lies in the nature of man and in the nature of God. As Creator, God formed man to be a vessel in which He could show forth His power and goodness. Man was not to have a fountain of life in himself, or strength, or happiness. The ever-living One was the Communicator to him of all that he needed each moment. Man's glory and blessedness was not to be independent, or dependent upon himself, but dependent on a God of such infinite riches and love. Man was to have the joy of receiving out of the fullness of God every moment. This was his blessedness as an unfallen creature.

When man fell from God, he became more dependent on Him. There was no hope of his recovery from his state of death except in God, His power, and His mercy. God alone began the work of redemption; God alone continues and carries it each moment in each individual believer. *We ourselves groan within ourselves, waiting for the adoption, that is to say, the redemption of our body* (Romans 8:23). Even in the regenerate man, there is no power of goodness in himself. He has and can have nothing that he does not receive; waiting on God is just as indispensable and must be just as continuous and unbroken as the breathing that maintains his natural life.

Because Christians do not understand their relationship to God as one of absolute poverty and helplessness, they have no sense of the need of absolute and unceasing dependence or the unspeakable blessedness of continual waiting on God. But when a believer begins to see it and consent to it, he must receive what God works each moment by the Holy Spirit. Then, waiting on God becomes his brightest hope and joy. *Being confident of this very thing, that he who has begun a good work in you will perfect it until the day of Jesus Christ* (Philippians 1:6).

As man understands how God, as God, as Infinite Love, delights to impart His own nature to His child as fully as He can, and how God is not weary of keeping charge of his life and strength, he wonders why he ever doubted that He was a God to be waited on all the day. This God unceasingly gives and works; His child unceasingly waits and receives – this is the blessed life.

Truly my soul waiteth upon God: from Him cometh my salvation. First we wait on God for salvation. Then we learn that salvation is what brings us to God and teaches us to wait on Him. Then we find what is better – that waiting on God is itself the highest salvation. It ascribes to Him the glory of being All; waiting is the experience that He is All to us. May God teach us the blessedness of waiting on Him.

My soul, wait thou only upon God!

Second Day

The Keynote of Life

I have waited for thy salvation, O LORD.
– Genesis 49:18 KJV

It is not easy to determine what Jacob meant with these words that he uttered in the midst of his prophecies about the future of his sons. But they do certainly indicate that his expectation for himself and his sons was from God alone. God's salvation was what he waited for – a salvation that God had promised and He alone could work out. Jacob knew he and his sons were under God's charge. Jehovah the everlasting God would show what His saving power is and what it would do through them. The words point to that wonderful history of redemption that was not yet finished and to the glorious future in eternity wherever it was leading. They suggest to us how there is no salvation but God's salvation, and how waiting on God for that, whether for our personal experience or for mankind in general, is our constant duty and our true blessedness.

Let us think of ourselves with that glorious salvation that God has wrought for us in Christ. Think of Him now purposing to work out and perfect us by His Spirit. Let us meditate until we realize that all participation of this great salvation, from moment to moment, must be the work of God Himself. Think of Paul's statement that *God would make known what is the riches of the glory of this mystery in the Gentiles, which is Christ in you, the hope of glory, whom we preach, warning every man and teaching in all wisdom that we may present every man perfect in Christ Jesus, in which I continue to labour, contending according to his operation, which he works in me mightily* (Colossians 1:27-29).

God cannot part with His grace, goodness, or strength as an external thing that He gives us, as He gives the raindrops from heaven. No, He can only give it, and we can only enjoy it, as He works it Himself directly and unceasingly. And the only reason that He does not work it more effectually and continuously is that we do not let Him. We hinder Him either by our indifference or by our self-effort, so He cannot do what He would like to do. What He asks of us in the way of surrender, obedience, desire, and trust is all included in this one word: *waiting* – waiting on Him and waiting for His salvation. It combines the deep sense of our entire helplessness to work what is divinely good and our perfect confidence that our God will work it all in His divine power.

Again, I say, let us meditate on the divine glory of the salvation that God purposes to work out in us until we know the truths it implies. Our heart is the scene of a divine operation more wonderful than creation. We can do as little towards the work as towards creating the world, except as God works in us to will and to do. God only asks us to yield, to consent, and to wait upon Him, and He will do it all. Let us meditate and be still, until we see how good and right and blessed it is that God alone does all. *Be still, and know that I am God; I will be exalted in the Gentiles, I will be exalted in the earth* (Psalm 46:10). Our soul will sink down in deep humility to say, *I have waited for thy salvation, O LORD.* And the deep, blessed background of all our praying and working will be, *Truly my soul waiteth upon God.*

The application of the truth to wider circles of influence, to those we labor among or intercede for, to the church of Christ around us or throughout the world, is not difficult. There can be no good except when God works; to wait upon God and have our hearts filled with faith in His working and to pray for His mighty power to come down, is our only wisdom. Oh, for the eyes of our heart to be opened to see God working in us and in others and to see how blessed it is to worship and to wait for His salvation!

Our private and public prayers are our chief expression of our relationship to God; it is chiefly in them that our waiting upon God is exercised. If our waiting begins by quieting the activities of the day and being still before God, we will see the salvation of God. If while waiting we bow and seek to see God in His universal and almighty operation, always ready to work all good, we will be strengthened. If our waiting yields itself to Him in the assurance that He is working and will work in us, we will have hope. If it maintains the place of humility and stillness, and surrenders until God's Spirit has quickened the faith that He will perfect His work, it will indeed become the strength and the joy of the soul, *for the joy of the LORD is your strength* (Nehemiah 8:10). Life will become one deep, blessed cry: *I have waited for thy salvation, O LORD.*

My soul, wait thou only upon God!

Third Day

The True Place of the Creature

These wait all upon thee, that thou may give them their food in due season. Thou givest unto them, they gather; thou openest thine hand, they are filled with good. – Psalm 104:27-28

I n praise of the Creator, this psalm speaks of the birds and the beasts of the forest, of the young lions and man going to his work, and of the great sea, wherein innumerable things creep, both small and great beasts. It sums up the relationship of all creation to its Creator and its continuous and universal dependence upon Him in the one statement: *These wait all upon thee.* Just as much as it was God's work to create, it is His work to maintain. As implausible as the idea is that the creature could create itself, so is the notion that it is left to provide for itself. The whole creation is ruled by the one unalterable law of *waiting upon God.*

The statement is the simple expression that for the sake of the creature alone, it was brought into existence, the very groundwork of its constitution. The one reason that God gave life to creatures was that in them He might prove and show His wisdom, power, and goodness – that in His being their life and happiness, He might pour forth unto them the riches of His goodness and power. And just as the purpose and nature of God is to be unceasingly the supplier of every desire in the creature, so the purpose and nature of the creature is to wait upon God – to receive from Him what He alone can give what He delights to give.

If we are to comprehend what *waiting on God* should be to the believer, to practice it, and to experience its blessedness, we must begin at the beginning and see the deep wisdom of the call that comes to us. We shall understand how our duty is no arbitrary command. We shall see how it is not only rendered necessary by our sin and helplessness, but it is also our restoration to our original destiny and our highest nobility – our true place and glory as creatures blessedly dependent on the all-glorious God.

When our eyes are opened to this precious truth, all nature will become a preacher and will remind us of the relationship that was founded in creation but now implemented in grace. As we read this psalm and learn to look upon all life in nature as continually maintained by God Himself, waiting on God will be realized as the very necessity of our being. As we think of the young lions and the ravens crying to Him, and the birds and the fishes and every insect waiting on Him until He gives them their food in due season, we shall see that it is the very nature and glory of God that He is a God who is to be waited on. Every thought of what nature is and what God is, will give new force to the call: *wait thou only upon God.*

These wait all upon thee, that thou may give. God is the One who gives all; let this faith enter deeply into our hearts. Before we fully understand all that is implied in our waiting upon God, and before we have even been able to cultivate the habit, let the truth enter our souls. Waiting on God, unceasing and entire dependence upon Him, is the one unalterable and all-comprehensive expression of the true relationship to the ever-blessed One in whom we live.

Let us resolve at once that it shall be the one characteristic of our life and worship – a continual, humble, truthful waiting upon God. We may rest assured that He who made us for Himself and gives Himself to us and in us will never disappoint us. In waiting on Him, we shall find rest and joy and strength and the supply of every need.

My soul, wait thou only upon God!

Fourth Day

Waiting for Supplies

The LORD upholds all that fall and raises up all those that are oppressed. The eyes of all wait upon thee, and thou givest them their food in due season. – Psalm 145:14-15

Psalm 104 is a psalm of creation, and the words, *These wait all upon thee*, were used with reference to the animal creation.

But in Psalm 145 we have a psalm of the kingdom, and *the eyes of all wait upon thee* appears to point specifically to the needs of God's saints, those who fall and those who are oppressed. What the universe and the animal creation does unconsciously, God's people are to do intelligently and voluntarily. Man is to be the interpreter of nature; he is to prove that there is nothing more noble or more blessed in the exercise of our free will than to use it in waiting upon God.

If an army has been sent to march into an enemy's country, and word is received that it is not advancing, at once the question is what may be the cause of delay. The answer will very often be, "Waiting for supplies." No stores of provisions, clothing, or ammunition have arrived; without these the army dare not proceed. It is no different in the Christian life; day by day, at every step, we need our supplies from above, and there is nothing so necessary as cultivation of that spirit of dependence on God and confidence in Him, which refuses to go on without the needed supply of grace and strength.

If the question is asked whether this is different from what we do when we pray, the answer is that there may be much praying but very little waiting on God. In praying, we are often occupied with ourselves, our own needs, and our own efforts. In waiting upon God, the first thought is of *the God upon whom we wait*. We enter His presence and feel we just need to be quiet, so that He, as God, can overshadow us with Himself. God longs to reveal Himself and to fill us with Himself. Waiting on God gives Him time to come to us in His way and divine power. It is at the time of prayer that we ought to set ourselves to embrace this spirit.

Before you pray, bow quietly before God to remember and realize who He is, how near He is, and how certainly He can and will help. Be still before Him, and allow His Holy Spirit to waken and stir your soul with the child-like disposition of absolute dependence and confident expectation. Wait upon God as a living Being, the living God, who notices you and longs to fill you with His salvation. Wait on God until you know you have met Him; prayer will then become very different.

And when you are praying, let there be intervals of

silence, reverent stillness of soul, in which you yield yourself to God in case He may desire to teach you or to work in you. Waiting on Him will become the most blessed part of prayer, and the blessing thus obtained will be doubly precious as the fruit of such fellowship with the Holy One. God has so ordained it in harmony with His holy nature and with ours that waiting on Him would be the honor we give Him. Let us bring Him the service gladly and truthfully; He will reward it abundantly.

The eyes of all wait upon thee, and thou givest them their food in due season. Dear soul, God provides in nature for the creatures He has made; how much more will He provide in grace for those He has redeemed! Learn to say of every desire, every failure, and every lack of needful grace: I have waited too little upon God, or He would have given me in due season all I needed. And then say:

My soul, wait thou only upon God!

Fifth Day

Waiting for Instruction

Show me thy ways, O LORD; teach me thy paths. Cause me to walk in thy truth and teach me: for thou art the God of my saving health; I have waited for thee all the day.
– Psalm 25:4-5

I spoke of an army on the point of entering an enemy's territories. The answer to the question as to the cause of delay was, "Waiting for supplies." The answer might also have been, "Waiting for instructions," or "Waiting for orders." If the last dispatch had not been received with the final orders of the commander-in-chief, the army would not dare to move. So it is in the Christian life: as necessary as the need for *waiting for supplies*, so is the need for *waiting for instructions*.

See how beautiful this comes out in Psalm 25:3 – *Yea, none that wait on thee shall be ashamed, let not my enemies triumph over me.*

The writer knew and loved God's law exceedingly,

and he meditated on that law day and night. But he knew that this was not enough. He knew that for the right spiritual comprehension of the truth, and for the right personal application of it to his own peculiar circumstances, he needed a direct divine teaching.

This psalm has at all times been a very peculiar one because of its reiterated expression of the felt need of the divine teaching and the childlike confidence that that teaching would be given. Study the psalm until your heart is filled with the two thoughts – the absolute need and the absolute certainty of divine guidance. These thoughts show how he can say, *I have waited for thee all the day.* Waiting for guidance and waiting for instruction all the day is a very blessed part of waiting upon God.

The Father in heaven is so interested in His child and so longs to have his life in His will and His love at every step that He is willing to keep his guidance in His own hand. He knows that we are unable to do what is holy and heavenly except as He works it in us, so His very demands become promises of what He will do in watching over and leading us all the day. Not only in special difficulties and times of perplexity, but also in the common course of everyday life, we may count upon Him to teach us His way and show us His path.

What is needed in us to receive this guidance? One thing: waiting for instructions, waiting on God. *I have waited for thee all the day.* In our times of prayer we want to give clear expression to our sense of need and our faith in His help. We want to become conscious of our ignorance of what God's way may be and the need of the divine light shining within us, if our way is to be as from the sun that shines more and more unto the perfect day. And we want to wait quietly before God in prayer until the deep, restful assurance fills us; it will be given – *the meek he will teach his way* (Psalm 25:9).

I have waited for thee all the day. The special surrender to the divine guidance in our seasons of prayer must prepare for and be followed up by the habitual looking upwards all the day. As simple as it is for one who has eyes to walk all the day in the light of the sun, so simple and delightful it can become to a soul practiced in waiting on God to walk all the day in the enjoyment of God's light and leading. What is needed to help us to such a life is just one thing: the real knowledge and faith of God as the only source of wisdom and goodness, who is ever ready and longing to be all that we can possibly require. Yes, our need is the one thing. If we could see our God in His love, and if we believe He waits to be gracious, to be our life, and to work all in us, then this waiting on God would become our highest joy, the natural and spontaneous response of our hearts to His great love and glory!

My soul, wait thou only upon God!

Sixth Day

For All Saints

*Yea, none that wait on thee shall be
ashamed.* – Psalm 25:3

In our meditation of today, let us each forget himself
and think of the great company of God, saints
throughout the world, who are all waiting on Him with
us. And let us all join in the fervent prayer for each
other: *Yea, none that wait on thee shall be ashamed.*

Just think for a moment of the waiting multitude
who need that prayer; how many sick and weary and
lonely to whom it seems their prayers are not answered,
and who sometimes fear that their hope will be put to
shame. Then think of how many servants of God –
ministers or missionaries, teachers or workers – whose
hopes in their work have been disappointed and whose
longings for power and blessing remain unsatisfied. How
many have heard of a life of rest and perfect peace, of
abiding light and fellowship, of strength and victory,
but cannot find the path.

With all these, they have not yet learned the secret of complete waiting upon God. They only need what we all need – the living assurance that waiting on God is never in vain. Remember all who are in danger of fainting or being weary and unite in the cry, *Yea, none that wait on thee shall be ashamed.*

If this intercession for all who wait on God becomes part of our waiting on Him for ourselves, we will bear each other's burdens and so fulfill the law of Christ. That element of unselfishness and love, which is the path to the highest blessing and the most complete communion with God, will be introduced into our waiting on God.

Love of the brethren and love of God are inseparably linked. In God, the love of His Son and of us are one: *That the love with which thou hast loved me may be in them* (John 17:26). In Christ, the love of the Father for Him and His love for us are one: *As the Father has loved me, so I have loved you* (John 15:9). In us, He asks that His love for us be ours for the brethren: *That ye love one another as I have loved you* (John 15:12). All the love of God and of Christ are inseparably linked to love of the brethren. And how can we prove and cultivate this love except by daily praying for each other? Christ did not seek to enjoy the Father's love for Himself; He passed it all on to us. All true seeking after God and His love for us will be inseparably linked to the thought and the love of our brethren in prayer for them.

Yea, none that wait on thee shall be ashamed. Twice in the twenty-fifth psalm David speaks of his waiting on God for himself, but here he thinks of all who wait on Him. May this message go to all God's tried and weary ones – there are more praying for them than they know. Let it stir them and us in our waiting to forget ourselves, to enlarge our hearts, and to say to the Father, *The eyes of all wait upon thee, and thou givest them their food in due season* (Psalm 145:15). Let it inspire us all with new courage, for who is there who is not at times ready to faint and be weary? *Yea, none that wait on thee shall be ashamed* is a promise in a prayer. *None that wait on thee shall be ashamed!* From many witnesses the cry comes to everyone who needs the help – brother, sister, weary one: *Wait for the LORD: be of good courage, and he shall strengthen thine heart; wait, I say, for the LORD* (Psalm 27:14). *Be of good courage and strengthen your hearts, all ye that wait in the LORD* (Psalm 31:24).

Blessed Father, we humbly beseech Thee, let none that wait on Thee be ashamed, no, not one. Some are weary, and the time of waiting appears long. And some are feeble and scarcely know how to wait. And some are so entangled in the effort of their prayers and their work that they think they can find no time to wait continually. Father, teach us all how to wait. Teach us to think of each other and pray for each other. Teach us to think of Thee, the God of all waiting ones. Father, let none that wait on Thee be ashamed. For Jesus' sake. Amen.

My soul, wait thou only upon God!

Seventh Day

A Plea in Prayer

Integrity and uprightness shall preserve me,
for I have waited for thee. – Psalm 25:21

For the third time in this psalm, we have the word *wait*. As before in verse 5, *I have waited for thee all the day*, so here, the believer appeals to God to remember that he is waiting for Him and looking for an answer. It is a great thing for a soul not only to wait upon God but also to be filled with such a consciousness that its whole spirit and position is that of waiting. Then in childlike confidence it can say, "Lord, Thou knowest I wait on Thee." It will prove a mighty plea in prayer and give ever-increasing boldness of expectation to claim the promise that *none that wait on thee shall be ashamed.*

The prayer in connection with the plea that is put forth here is one of great importance in the spiritual life. If we draw near to God, it must be with a true heart. There must be perfect integrity and wholeheartedness in our dealing with God, as we read in the next psalm,

*Judge me, O LORD, for I have walked in my integrity; . .
. as for me, I will walk in my integrity* (Psalm 26:1, 11).
There must be perfect uprightness or single-heartedness
before God, as the psalmist asked Him to *extend . . .
thy righteousness to the upright in heart* (Psalm 36:10).
The soul must know that it allows nothing sinful and
nothing doubtful if it is to meet the Holy One and
receive His full blessing; it must be with a heart wholly
and singly given up to His will. The whole spirit that
animates us in the waiting must do so with *integrity
and uprightness* – You see that I desire to come so to
You; You know I am looking to You to work integrity
and uprightness perfectly in me; let them *preserve me,
for I have waited for thee* (Psalm 25:21).

With our first attempt to live life completely and
always waiting on God, we may discover how much
that perfect integrity is lacking. This will just be one of
the blessings that the waiting was meant to produce. A
soul cannot seek close fellowship with God or attain the
abiding consciousness of waiting on Him all the day
without an honest and entire surrender to all His will.

For I have waited for thee. These words not only
refer to the prayer of our text but also to every prayer.
To use them often will be a great blessing to ourselves.
Let us therefore study the words until we know all their
meanings. It must be clear to us what we are waiting
for. There may be very different things. It may mean
waiting for God in our times of prayer to take His place
as God to work in us the sense of His holy presence
and nearness. It may be a special petition to which we
are expecting an answer. We might be waiting for our

whole inner life to experience God's power. Our eyes may be looking for God's hand in the whole state of His church and saints or some part of His work. It is good that we sometimes recognize what the things are that we are waiting for, and as we say to each of them, *I have waited for thee*, we shall be emboldened to claim the answer, *for I have waited for thee all the day.*

It must also be clear to us on whom we are waiting. We do not wait on an idol, a god that we have made an image of by our conceptions of what He is. No, we wait on the living God, such as He really is in His great glory, His infinite holiness, His power, wisdom, and goodness, and in His love and nearness. The presence of a beloved or a dreaded master wakens the whole attention of the servant who waits on him. It is the presence of God, as He makes Himself known in Christ by His Holy Spirit and keeps the soul under its covering and shadow that will waken and strengthen the true waiting spirit. Let us be still, and wait, and worship until we know how near He is and then say, *I have waited for thee.*

Let it be very clear that *we are waiting.* Let that become so much our consciousness that the utterance comes spontaneously, *I have waited all the day; I have waited for thee.* This will indeed imply sacrifice and separation, a soul entirely given up to God, its only joy. This waiting on God has hardly been acknowledged as the only true Christianity. And yet, if it is true that God alone is goodness and joy and love, that our highest blessedness is in having as much of God as we can, and that Christ has redeemed us for God and made a life of continual abiding in His presence possible, nothing less ought to satisfy us than to be always breathing this blessed atmosphere, *I wait on Thee.*

My soul, wait thou only on God!

Eighth Day

Strong and of Good Courage

Wait for the LORD; be strong, and let your heart take courage; yea, wait for the LORD!
– Psalm 27:14 RSV

The psalmist had just said, *I had fainted unless I had believed to see the goodness of the LORD in the land of the living* (Psalm 27:13). If it had not been for his faith in God, his heart would have fainted. But in the confident assurance in God that faith gives, he urged himself and us to remember one thing above all – to wait upon God. *Wait for the LORD; be strong, and let your heart take courage, yea, wait for the LORD!* One of the chief needs in our waiting upon God, one of the deepest secrets of its blessedness and blessing, is a quiet, confident persuasion that it is not in vain; it is courage to believe that God will hear and help. We are waiting on a God who could never disappoint His people.

Be strong and of a good courage (Joshua 1:9). These

words are frequently found in connection with some great and difficult enterprise or in the prospect of combat with the power of strong enemies and the utter insufficiency of all human strength. Is waiting on God a work so difficult that these words are needed: *Be strong, and let your heart take courage*? Yes, indeed. The deliverance for which we often wait is from enemies when we are helpless. The blessings for which we plead are spiritual and unseen, things impossible with men but heavenly, supernatural, divine realities. Our heart may well faint and fail. Our souls are so seldom accustomed to fellowship with God, the God on whom we wait, that He often appears to hide Himself. We who have to wait are often tempted to fear that we do not wait correctly, that our faith is too weak, that our desire is not as righteous or earnest as it should be, or that our surrender is not complete. Amid all these causes of fear or doubt, how blessed to hear the voice of God say, *Wait for the LORD; be strong, and let your heart take courage; yea, wait for the LORD!* Let nothing in heaven, on earth, or in hell – let nothing keep you from waiting on your God in full assurance, so your waiting is not in vain.

The one lesson our text teaches us is this: when we set ourselves to wait on God, we should resolve that we will wait with the most confident expectation of God meeting and blessing us. We should make up our minds to do this, for nothing was ever so sure as the untold and unexpected blessing that waiting on God will bring us. We are accustomed to judge God and His work in us by what we feel. Therefore, there is the great probability that when we cultivate the waiting on

Him, we will be discouraged, because we do not find any special blessing from it. The message that comes to us is this: above everything, when we wait on God, we need to do so in the spirit of abounding hopefulness. It is God in His glory, in His power, and in His love whom we are waiting on, who longs to bless us.

If you say that you are afraid of deceiving yourself with vain hope because you do not see or feel any reason in your present state for such special expectations, my answer is that God is the One who provides the justification for you to expect great things. Oh, do learn the lesson. You are not going to wait on yourself to see what you feel and what changes come to you. You are going to *wait on God*, to know first what He is and then what He will do. The whole duty and blessedness of waiting on God has its root in this – He is such a blessed Being, full to overflowing of goodness and power and life and joy that we, however wretched, cannot for any time come into contact with Him without that life and power secretly, silently entering into us and blessing us.

God is Love! That is the one and all-sufficient reason for your expectation. Love seeks out its own: God's love is His delight to impart Himself and His blessedness to His children. Come, and however weak you feel, wait in His presence. As a weak, sickly invalid is brought out into the sunshine to let its warmth go through him, come with all that is dark and cold in you into the sunshine of God's holy, omnipotent love, and sit and wait there with the one thought: here I am, in the sunshine of His love. As the sun does its work in the weak one who seeks its rays, God will do His work in you. Oh, trust Him completely. *Wait for the LORD; be strong, and let your heart take courage; yea, wait for the LORD!*

My soul, wait thou only upon God!

Ninth Day

Waiting with the Heart

*Be strong, and let your heart take
courage, all you who wait for the LORD!*
– Psalm 31:24 RSV

The words are nearly the same as in our last
meditation. But I gladly return to them to press
home a much-needed lesson for all who desire to learn
what waiting for God is. The lesson is this: It is *with
the heart* that we must wait for God. *Let your heart
take courage.* All our waiting depends upon the state
of the heart. As a man's heart is, so is he before God.
We can advance no further or deeper into the holy
place of God's presence than our heart is prepared for
by the Holy Spirit. The message is, *Let your heart take
courage, all you who wait for the LORD.*

The truth appears so simple: some may ask, doesn't
everyone admit this? And where is the need for insisting
on it specifically? It is because many Christians have
no sense of the great difference between the religion of

the mind and the religion of the heart, and the former is more diligently developed than the latter. They don't know how infinitely greater the heart is than the mind. This is one of the chief reasons for the feebleness of our Christian life; only as this is understood can we wait on God to bring its full blessing.

A text in Proverbs may help us to comprehend this. Speaking of a life in the fear and favor of God, Solomon said, *Trust in the LORD with all thine heart and lean not unto thine own understanding* (Proverbs 3:5). In all religion, we have to use these two powers. The mind must gather knowledge from God's Word and prepare the food for the heart so the inner life can be nourished. But here is a terrible danger: leaning on our own understanding and trusting in our comprehension of divine things. People imagine that if they are occupied with the truth, the spiritual life will be strengthened automatically.

But this is by no means the case. The understanding deals with concepts and images of divine things, but it cannot reach the real life of the soul. Hence the command: *Trust in the LORD with all thine heart and lean not unto thine own understanding.* It is with the heart that man believes and connects with God (Romans 10:10). It is in the heart that God has given His Spirit as the presence and power of God working in us. In our religion, it is the heart that must trust and love and worship and obey. My mind is not able to create or maintain the spiritual life within me; the heart must wait for God to work in me.

Even in the physical life this is so. My reason may tell

mc what to eat and drink and how the food nourishes me. But in the eating, my reason can do nothing; the body has its organs for that special purpose. Reason may tell me what God's Word says, but it can do nothing to feed the soul on the Bread of Life; the heart alone can do this by its faith and trust in God. A man may study the nature and effects of food or sleep; when he wants to eat or sleep, he sets aside his thoughts and study, and he uses the power of eating or sleeping. Even so, when the Christian has studied or heard God's Word, he must cease from his thoughts and put no trust in them; he must waken his heart to open itself before God and seek the living fellowship with Him.

This is the blessedness of waiting upon God: that I confess the deficiency of all my thoughts and efforts and bow my heart before Him in holy silence, as I trust Him to renew and strengthen His work in me. And this is the lesson of our text: *Let your heart take courage, all you who wait for the LORD.* Remember the difference between knowing with the mind and believing with the heart. Beware of the temptation to lean on your own understanding with its clear, strong thoughts. They only help you to know what the heart must get from God. Your thoughts are only images and shadows. *Let your heart take courage, all you who wait for the LORD.* Present it before Him as that wonderful part of your spiritual nature in which God reveals Himself and by which you can know Him. Cultivate the greatest confidence that God is working there by His Holy Spirit. Let your heart wait at times in perfect silence and quiet; in its hidden depths, God will work.

Be sure of this, and just wait on Him. Continually give your whole heart with its secret workings into God's hands. He wants the heart and takes it, and as He dwells in it, *be strong, and let your heart take courage, all you who wait for the LORD.*

My soul, wait thou only upon God!

Tenth Day

Waiting in Humble Fear and Hope

Behold, the eye of the LORD is upon those that fear him, upon those that wait for his mercy to deliver their souls from death and to keep them alive in the famine. Our soul waited for the LORD; he is our help and our shield. Therefore our heart shall rejoice in him because we have trusted in the name of his holiness. Let thy mercy, O LORD, be upon us, according as we have waited upon thee. – Psalm 33:18-22

God's eye is upon His people; their eye is upon Him. As we wait upon God, our eye looks up to Him and meets His eye looking down on us. This is the blessedness of waiting upon God. It takes our eyes and thoughts away from ourselves, from our needs and desires, and occupies us with our God. We worship Him in His glory and love, with His all-seeing eye watching over us, so that He may supply our every need. Let us consider this wonderful meeting between God and His people and remember what we are taught about those on whom God's eye rests and on whom our eye rests.

The eye of the LORD is upon those that fear him, upon those that wait for his mercy. Fear and the hope of waiting are generally thought to be in conflict with each other. In the presence and worship of God, they are found side by side in perfect and beautiful harmony. This is because all apparent contradictions are reconciled in God Himself. Righteousness and peace, judgment and mercy, holiness and love, infinite power and infinite gentleness, a majesty that is exalted above all heaven and a condescension that bows low, meet and kiss each other. Indeed, a fear exists that has torment and is cast out entirely by perfect love. But there is a fear that is found in the very heavens. In the song of Moses and the Lamb they sing:

Who shall not fear thee, O Lord, and magnify thy name? (Revelation 15:4). *And a voice came out of the throne, saying, Praise our God, all ye his slaves and ye that fear him* (Revelation 19:5). Let us in our waiting ever seek to *fear this glorious and fearful name; I AM thy God* (Deuteronomy 28:58). The lower we bow before His holiness in holy fear and adoring awe, in deep reverence and humble self-abasement, as even the angels veil their faces before the throne, the more His holiness will rest upon us. Our soul will be filled to have God reveal Himself to us, and the deeper we enter into the truth *that no flesh should glory in his presence*, it will be given to us to see His glory (1 Corinthians 1:29).

The eye of the LORD is upon those that fear him, upon those that wait for his mercy.

The true fear of God will never keep us back from the waiting, the hope, but it will stimulate and strengthen it. The lower we bow, the deeper we feel we have nothing to hope in except His mercy. The lower we bow, the nearer God will come and make our hearts bold to trust Him. Let every exercise of waiting, our whole habit of waiting on God, be infused with abounding hope – a hope as bright and boundless as God's mercy. The fatherly kindness of God is such that we may confidently hope in His mercy whatever the state in which we come to Him.

Such are God's waiting ones. And now, think of the God on whom we wait. *The eye of the LORD is upon those that fear him, upon those that wait for his mercy to deliver their souls from death and to keep them alive in famine.* His watchful eye is not to prevent the danger of death and famine, which are often needed to stimulate men to wait on Him, but to deliver and to keep them alive. The dangers are often very real and dark, and the situation, whether in the physical or spiritual life, may appear to be utterly hopeless. But there is always one hope: *God's eye is on them.*

That eye sees the danger and in tender love sees His trembling, waiting child; He sees the moment when the heart is ripe for the blessing and the way in which it is to come. This living, mighty God, oh, let's fear Him and hope in His mercy. And let us humbly but boldly say, *Our soul waited for the LORD; he is our help and*

*our shield. . . . Let thy mercy, O LORD, be upon us,
according as we have waited upon thee.*

Oh, the blessedness of waiting on such a God! A
very present help in every time of trouble; a shield and
defense against every danger (Psalm 46:1). Children of
God, won't you learn to bow in complete helplessness
and powerlessness and to wait in stillness to see the
salvation of God? In the utmost spiritual famine, and
when death appears inevitable, wait on God. He deliv-
ers, and He keeps alive. Repeat the psalm not only in
solitude, but repeat it also to each other – the psalm
that speaks not of one but of all God's people: *Our
soul waited for the LORD; he is our help and our shield.*
Strengthen and encourage each other in the exercise
of waiting, so that each may not only say of himself,
but also of his brethren: *this is the LORD, whom we
have waited for, we will be glad and rejoice in his saving
health* (Isaiah 25:9).

My soul, wait thou only upon God!

Eleventh Day

Waiting Patiently

Be silent before the LORD and wait patiently for him; . . . those that wait for the LORD, they shall inherit the earth (Psalm 37:7, 9)

In your patience ye shall possess your souls (Luke 21:19). *For patience is necessary* (Hebrews 10:36). *The patience finishes the work, that ye may be perfect and entire* (James 1:4).

S uch words of the Holy Spirit show us what an important element patience is in the Christian life and character. Nowhere is there a better place for developing or displaying it than in waiting on God. This is where we discover how impatient we are and what our impatience means. We confess at times that we are impatient with men and circumstances that hinder us, or with ourselves and our slow progress in the Christian life. If we set ourselves to wait upon God, we shall find that we are impatient with Him because He does not do our bidding as soon as we wish. In waiting upon God, our eyes are opened to believe in His wise and sovereign will and to see that the sooner we yield to it, the more surely His blessing can come to us.

So then it is not of him that wills, nor of him that runs, but of God that has mercy (Romans 9:16). We have as little power to increase or strengthen our spiritual life as we had to originate it. We were *not born of blood, nor of the will of flesh, nor of the will of man, but of God* (John 1:13). Even so, our willing and running, our desire and effort, profit nothing; all is *of God that has mercy.* All the exercises of the spiritual life, our reading and praying, our willing and doing, have great value. But they can go no further than this – that they point the way and prepare us in humility to look to and depend on God Himself, and in patience to wait for His good time and mercy. The waiting teaches us our absolute dependence upon God's mighty working and empowers us in perfect patience. We place ourselves at His disposal. They *that wait for the LORD, they shall inherit the earth* – the promised land and its blessing. The heirs must wait; they can afford to wait.

Be silent before the LORD and wait patiently for him. Or, be still before the Lord. It is resting in the Lord, in His will, His promise, His faithfulness, and His love that makes patience easy. And the resting in Him is nothing but being silent or still before Him. It is having our thoughts and wishes, and our fears and hopes hushed into calm and quiet in that great peace of God that passes all understanding. That peace keeps the heart and mind when we are anxious for anything, because we have made our request known to Him (Philippians 4:7). The rest, the silence, the stillness, and the patient waiting, all find their strength and joy in God Himself.

The needs, the reasonableness, and the blessedness of patience will be opened up to the waiting soul. Our patience will be seen as the counterpart of God's patience. He longs to bless us much more than we desire it. But, as the farmer has patience for the fruit to ripen, so God bears with our slowness and waits for us. Let us remember this and wait patiently for each promise and every answer to prayer; the word is true that *I the LORD will hasten it in its time* (Isaiah 60:22).

Be silent before the LORD and wait patiently for him. Yes, *for* Him. Don't only seek for help or the gift; you need to seek Him and wait for Him. Give God His glory by resting in Him, by trusting Him fully, by waiting patiently for Him. This patience honors Him and leaves Him on the throne as God to do His work; it yields self wholly into His hands. It lets God be God. If your waiting is for some special request, wait patiently. If your waiting is an exercise of the spiritual life seeking to know and have more of God, wait patiently. Whether it is in the shorter, specific periods of waiting or as the continuous habit of the soul, rest in the Lord; *be silent before the LORD and wait patiently. Those that wait for the LORD, they shall inherit the earth.*

My soul, wait thou only upon God!

Twelfth Day

Keeping His Ways

*Wait on the LORD and keep his way, and
he shall exalt thee to inherit the earth.*
– Psalm 37:34

I f we desire to find a man whom we long to meet, we
inquire about the places where he might be found and
what his ways are. When waiting on God, we need to
be careful that we keep His ways; we can never expect
to find Him apart from these. *Thou didst come out to
meet him that with rejoicing had worked righteousness.
In thy ways they remembered thee* (Isaiah 64:5). We may
be sure that God is never to be found except in His
ways. And by the soul who seeks and patiently waits,
He is always most surely to be found there. *Wait on
the LORD and keep his way, and he shall exalt thee.*

How close the connection is between the two parts:
Wait on the LORD has to do with worship and disposi-
tion, and *keep his way* deals with our walk and work.
The outer life must be in harmony with the inner; the

inner must be the inspiration and the strength for the outer. Our God has made His ways for our conduct known in His Word, and He invites our confidence for His grace and help in our heart. If we do not keep His ways, our waiting on Him can bring no blessing. The surrender to obedience to all His will is the secret of access to all the blessings of His fellowship.

Notice how strongly this comes out in the psalm. It speaks of the evildoer who prospers in his way and calls on the believer not to fret himself (Psalm 37:7). When we see men around us who are prosperous and happy while they forsake God's ways, and we are left in difficulty or suffering, we are in danger of fretting at what appears so unjust and then turning to seek our prosperity in their path. The psalm says, *Do not be angry* (verse 1); *wait in the LORD and do good* (verse 3). *Be silent before the LORD and wait patiently for him* (verse 7); *cease from anger and forsake wrath* (verse 8). *Depart from evil, and do good* (verse 27); *the LORD . . . does not forsake his merciful ones* (verse 28). *The righteous shall inherit the earth* (verse 29).

The law of his God is in his heart; therefore none of his steps shall slide (Psalm 37:31). And then this follows: *Wait on the LORD and keep his way.* If you do what God asks you to do, God will do more than you can ask of Him.

Let no one give in to the fear and claim that he cannot keep His ways. This robs one of all confidence. True, you don't have the strength yet to keep all His ways, but you can keep those for which you have already received strength. Surrender yourself willingly to keep all God's ways in the strength which will come from waiting on Him. Give up your whole being to God without reserve and without doubt; He will prove Himself God to you and work in you that which is pleasing in His sight through Jesus Christ. Keep His ways as you know them in the Word. Keep His ways as nature teaches them in always doing what appears right. Keep His ways as Providence points them out. Keep His ways as the Holy Spirit suggests. Don't think of waiting on God while you say you are not willing to work in His way. However weak you feel, just be willing, and He who has worked to will, will work to *do* by His power.

Wait on the LORD and keep his way.

It may be that the consciousness of shortcomings and sin makes our text look more like a hindrance than a help in waiting on God. Don't let it be so. Haven't we said more than once that the very starting point and groundwork of this waiting is utter and absolute ineffectiveness? Why not come with everything evil you feel in yourself – every memory of unwillingness, unwatchfulness, unfaithfulness, and all that causes such unceasing self-condemnation? Put your power in God's omnipotence and find your deliverance by waiting on God.

Your failure has been due to one thing: you sought to conquer and obey in your own strength. Come and bow before God until you learn that He is the God who alone is good and alone can work any good thing. Believe that in yourself and all that nature can do, there is no true power. Be content to receive the working of His mighty grace and life. Waiting on God will become the renewal of your strength to run in His ways and not be weary, to walk in His paths and never faint (Isaiah 40:31). *Wait on the LORD and keep his way* will be command and promise together.

My soul, wait thou only upon God!

Thirteenth Day

Waiting for More than We Know

And now, Lord, what shall I wait for? My hope is in thee. Deliver me from all my rebellions. – Psalm 39:7-8

There may be times when we don't know what we are waiting for. Other times we think we do know, even though it would be good for us to realize that we don't know what to ask as we ought. God is able to do for us exceeding abundantly above what we ask or think, and we are in danger of limiting Him when we confine our desires and prayers to our own thoughts. It is great to proclaim what our psalm says: *And now, Lord, what shall I wait for?* I scarcely know or can tell; this only can I say – *My hope is in thee.*

How we see this limiting of God in the case of Israel! When Moses promised them meat in the wilderness, they doubted and said, *Can God furnish a table in the wilderness? Behold, he smote the rock that the waters gushed out, and the streams overflowed; can he give bread also? can he provide flesh for his people?* (Psalm 78:19-20). If they had been asked whether God could provide streams in the desert, they would have answered yes. God had done it; He could do it again.

But when the thought came of God doing something new, they limited Him; their expectation could not rise above their experience or their own thoughts of what was possible. Likewise, we may limit God by our idea of what He has promised or is able to do. We must beware of limiting the Holy One of Israel in our prayers. Let us believe that the promises of God we plead for have a divine meaning, infinitely beyond our thoughts of them. Let us believe that in a power and an abundance of grace, His fulfillment of them can be beyond our understanding. And let us therefore cultivate the habit of waiting on God, not only for what we think we need, but also for all that His grace and power will do for us.

In every true prayer two hearts are involved. The one is your heart with its little, dark, human thoughts of what you need and what God can do. The other is God's great heart with its infinite, divine purposes of blessing. What do you think? To which of these two should the larger place be given in your approach to Him? Undoubtedly, to the heart of God. Everything depends upon knowing and being occupied with that, but how little this is done. Waiting on God is meant to teach this. Think about God's wonderful love and redemption; think about what these words mean to Him. Confess how little you understand what God is willing to do for you, and each time you pray, say, *And now, Lord, what shall I wait for?* My heart doesn't know. God's heart knows and waits to give. *My hope is in thee.* Wait on God to do more than you can ask or think.

Apply this to the prayer that follows: *Deliver me from all my rebellions.* You may have prayed to be delivered from temper, pride, or self-will. It seems to be in vain. Might it not be that you have had your own thoughts about the way or the extent of God's answer, or that you have not waited on the God of glory to do for you according to the riches of His glory what has not entered the heart of man to imagine?

Learn to worship God as the God who does wonders, who wishes to prove in you that He can do something supernatural and divine. Bow before Him, and wait upon Him, until your soul realizes that you are in the hands of a divine and almighty worker. Consent to know only what and how He will work; expect it to be something altogether godlike, something to be waited for in deep humility and received only by His divine power. Let the *And now, Lord, what shall I wait for? My hope is in thee* become the spirit of every longing and every prayer. He will do His work in His time.

Dear soul, in waiting on God you may often be weary, because you hardly know what to expect. Be of good courage – this ignorance is often one of the best signs. He is teaching you to leave everything in His hands and to wait on Him alone. *Wait for the LORD: be of good courage, and he shall strengthen thine heart; wait, I say, for the LORD.*

My soul, wait thou only upon God!

Fourteenth Day

A New Song

I waited patiently for the LORD, and he inclined unto me and heard my cry. And he has put a new song in my mouth, even praise unto our God. – Psalm 40:1, 3

Listen to the testimony of one who can speak from experience of the sure and blessed outcome of patient waiting upon God. True patience is foreign to our self-confident nature; it is indispensable in our waiting upon God; this element of true faith is so essential that we may once again meditate on what the Word teaches.

The word *patience* is derived from the Latin word for *suffering*. It suggests the thought of being under the constraint of some power from which we would gladly be free. At first we submit against our will; experience teaches us that when it is useless to resist, patient endurance is our wisest choice. In waiting on God, it is of infinite consequence that we not only submit because we are compelled to, but also because we lovingly and joyfully consent to be in the hands of our blessed Father.

Patience then becomes our highest blessedness and our highest grace. It honors God and gives Him time to have His way with us. It is the highest expression of our faith in His goodness and faithfulness. It brings the soul perfect rest in the assurance that God is carrying on His work. Patience is the token of our full consent that God should deal with us in such a way and time as He thinks best. True patience is the losing of our self-will in His perfect will.

Such patience is needed for the true and complete waiting on God. Such patience is the growth and fruit of our first lessons in the school of waiting. To many it appears strange how difficult it is to wait upon God. The great stillness of soul before God that sinks into its own helplessness and waits for Him to reveal Himself does not happen immediately. The deep humility that is afraid to let its own will or strength work anything, except as God works to will and to do, comes slowly. The meekness that is content to be and to know nothing, except as God gives His light, develops with time. The entire resignation of the will that only wants to be a vessel in which His holy will can move and mold occurs over a lifetime. None of these elements of perfect patience are found at once. They will come gradually as the soul maintains its position and says, *Truly my soul waiteth upon God: from him cometh my salvation. He only is my rock and my salvation* (Psalm 62:1-2 KJV).

Have you ever noticed what proof we have that patience is a grace for which very special grace is given? Note these words of Paul: *strengthened with all might, according to the power of his glory unto all* – all what? – *all patience and longsuffering with joyfulness* (Colossians 1:11). Yes, we need to be strengthened with all God's might and that according to the measure of His glorious power, if we are to wait on God in all patience. God reveals Himself in us as our life and strength that enable us with perfect patience to leave everything in His hands. If any are inclined to depression because they don't have such patience, let them be of good courage; it is in the course of our weak and imperfect waiting that God Himself strengthens us and works out in us the patience of the saints by His hidden power. He works the patience of Christ Himself in us.

Listen to the voice of one who was deeply tried: *I waited patiently for the LORD, and he inclined unto me and heard my cry.* Hear what he passed through: *He brought me up also out of the pit of hopelessness, out of the miry clay and set my feet upon a rock and straightened my steps. And He has put a new song in my mouth, even praise unto our God* (Psalm 40:2-3). Patient waiting upon God brings a rich reward, and the deliverance is sure. God Himself will put a new song into your mouth. O Christian! Don't be impatient – whether it is in the exercise of prayer and worship that you find it difficult to wait, or in the delay with respect to definite requests, or in the fulfilling of your heart's desire for the revelation of God Himself in a deeper spiritual life. Fear not, but rest in the Lord, and wait patiently for Him. If you sometimes feel as if patience is not your gift, then remember *it is* God's gift: *The Lord direct your hearts into the love of God, and into the patient waiting for Christ* (2 Thessalonians 3:5 KJV). The Lord directs your heart into the patience with which you are to wait on God; He Himself will guide you.

My soul, wait thou only upon God!

Waiting for His Counsel

They soon forgot his works; they waited not for his counsel. – Psalm 106:13

This is said of the sin of God's people in the wilderness. He had wonderfully redeemed them, and He was prepared to supply their every need. But when the time of need came, *they waited not for his counsel.* They didn't think about the almighty God who was their Leader and Provider; they didn't ask what His plans might be. They simply thought the thoughts of their own hearts and tempted and provoked God by their unbelief. *They waited not for his counsel.*

This has been the sin of God's people in all ages. In the land of Canaan in the days of Joshua, the only three failures we read about were due to this one sin. In going up against Ai, in making a covenant with the Gibeonites, and in settling down without conquering the whole land, *they waited not for his counsel* (Joshua 7; 9; 23; Judges 2:1-2). Even a mature believer is in danger from this most subtle of temptations – taking God's Word and thinking his own thoughts without waiting for His counsel. Let's take the warning and see what Israel teaches us. Let's especially regard this not only as a warning against danger that the individual is exposed to, but also as one against danger that all God's people experience and need to be on their guard against.

Our whole relationship to God is ruled in that His will is to be done in us and by us as it is in heaven. He has promised to make known His will to us by His Spirit, the Guide into all truth. Our position should be that of waiting for His counsel as the only guide for our thoughts and actions. In our church worship, in our prayer meetings, in our conventions, in all our gatherings as managers, directors, committees, or helpers in any work for God, our first objective should be to determine the mind of God. God always works according to the counsel of His will; the more that counsel of His will is sought, found, and honored, the more God will do His work for us and through us in a mighty way.

The great danger in all assemblies is that in our consciousness of having our Bible, our past experience of God's leading, our sound doctrine, and our honest desire to do God's will, we trust in these and do not realize that we need and may have heavenly guidance with every step. There may be elements of God's will, application of God's Word, experience of the close presence and leading of God, and manifestations of the power of His Spirit that we know nothing of as yet.

God is willing to open these up to the souls who will

allow Him to have His way and wait for Him to make it known. When we come together and praise God for all He has done and taught and given, we may at the same time limit Him by not expecting greater things. Even after God had given water out of the rock, the Israelites did not trust Him for bread. While we think that we know and trust the power of God for what we may expect, we may hinder Him by not giving Him time or cultivating the habit of waiting for His counsel.

The most solemn duty of a minister is to teach the people to wait upon God. Why was it that in the house of Cornelius, when *Peter yet spoke these words, the Holy Spirit fell on all those who heard the word* (Acts 10:44)? They had said, *we are all here present before God to hear all things that are commanded thee of God* (Acts 10:33). We may come together to give and to listen to the most earnest exposition of God's truth with little spiritual profit if there is no waiting for God's counsel.

In all our gatherings, we need to believe in the Holy Spirit as the Guide and Teacher of God's saints, as they wait to be led by Him into the things which God has prepared, and the heart cannot conceive of.

The assemblies of God's saints must cultivate more stillness of soul to realize God's presence, more consciousness of ignorance of God's plans, more faith that God has greater things to show us, and more expectation that He Himself will be revealed in new glory. These must be the marks of the assemblies if they want to avoid the reproach, *They waited not for his counsel.*

My soul, wait thou only upon God!

Waiting for His Light in the Heart

I have waited for the LORD, my soul has waited, and for his word I have waited. My soul has waited for the Lord more than those that watch for the morning: I say, more than those that watch for the morning. – Psalm 130:5-6

The morning light is often waited for with intense longing by the mariners in a shipwrecked vessel, by a traveler in a dangerous country at nighttime, or by an army that finds itself surrounded by an enemy. The morning light will show what hope of escape there may be. The morning may bring life and liberty. Likewise, the saints of God have longed for the light of His countenance more than watchmen long for the morning. More than watchmen for the morning, they have said, *My soul has waited for the Lord.* Can we say that too? Our waiting on God can have no higher purpose than simply having His light shine on us, in us, and through us all the day.

God is light; God is a sun. Paul said, *God, who commanded the light to shine out of darkness, has shined in our hearts to bring forth the light.* What light? *The light of the knowledge of the clarity of God in the face of Jesus Christ* (2 Corinthians 4:6). Just as the sun shines its beautiful, life-giving light on and into our earth, so God shines into our hearts the light of His glory and His love through Christ His Son. Our heart is meant to have that light filling and delighting it all the day. It can have it, because God is our sun. It is written, *Thy sun shall set no more* (Isaiah 60:20). God's love shines on us without ceasing.

But can we indeed enjoy it all the day? We can. But how can we? Let nature give us the answer. Those beautiful trees and flowers with all this green grass – what do they do to keep the sun shining on them? They do nothing; they simply bask in the sunshine when it comes. The sun is millions of miles away, but its own light and joy comes over all that distance, and the tiniest flower that lifts its little head upward is met by the same exuberance of light and blessing as what floods the widest landscape. We don't have to worry about the light we need for our day's work; the sun provides and shines the light around us all day. We simply expect it, receive it, and enjoy it.

The only difference between nature and grace is that what the trees and the flowers do unconsciously as they drink in the blessing of the light, is to be a voluntary and loving acceptance with us. Faith, simple faith in God's Word and love, will open the eyes and the heart to receive and enjoy the unspeakable glory of His grace. As the trees stand and grow day by day and month by month into beauty and fruitfulness, we need to welcome whatever sunshine may come as the highest exercise of our Christian life – to abide in the light of God and let Him fill us with the life and the brightness He brings.

And if you ask if it can really be that I can rejoice in God's light all day just as naturally and heartily as I recognize and rejoice in the beauty of a bright, sunny morning – yes, it can, indeed. From my breakfast table I look out on a beautiful valley with trees and vineyards and mountains. In our spring and autumn months, the light in the morning is exquisite, and we almost invariably say, how beautiful! And the question arises: Is the light of the sun the only source to bring such continual beauty and joy? Is there no provision for the light of God to be an unceasing source of joy and gladness? There is, indeed, if the soul will be still and wait on Him – just let God shine.

Dear Christian, learn to wait on the Lord more than watchers wait for the morning. Everything within you may feel very dark, but isn't that the best reason for waiting for the light of God? The first beginnings of light may be just enough to discover the darkness and painfully humble you because of sin. Can't you trust the light to expel the darkness? Believe it will. Just bow in stillness before God and wait on Him to shine into you. In humble faith, profess that God is light, infinitely brighter and more beautiful than that of the sun. God the Father is light. God the Son is the eternal and incomprehensible light. God the Holy Spirit is the concentrated, embodied, and manifested light. The Spirit is the light that enters, dwells, and shines in our hearts. God is light and shines in my heart.

Sometimes I have been so occupied with my thoughts and efforts that I haven't opened the shutters to let His light in. Unbelief has kept it out. I bow in faith: God is shining His light into my heart – the God of whom Paul wrote, *God has shined in our hearts*, is my God. What would I think of a sun that could not shine? What would I think of a God who does not shine? No, God shines! God is light! I will take time, be still, and rest in the light of God. My eyes are weak, and the windows are not clean, but I will wait on the Lord. The light does shine; the light will shine in me and make me full of light. I will learn to walk in the light and joy of God all day. *My soul has waited for the Lord more than those that watch for the morning.*

My soul, wait thou only upon God!

Seventeenth Day

Waiting in Times of Darkness

*I will wait for the LORD, who hid his face
from the house of Jacob, and I will look for
him.* – Isaiah 8:17

Isaiah was a servant of God who waited upon Him,
not on behalf of himself but for his people from
whom God was hiding His face. It suggests how our
waiting upon God, though it begins with our personal
needs, our desire for His revelation to us, or the answer
to personal petitions, does not need to stop there. We
may walk in the full light of God's countenance, and
God may hide His face from His people around us. Far
from being content to think that this is nothing but the
punishment for their sin or the consequence of their
indifference, we are called to think of their sad state
with tender hearts and wait on God on their behalf.

The privilege of waiting upon God is one that brings
great responsibility. Even as Christ used His place of
privilege and honor as intercessor when He entered

God's presence, so we must use our access for our less-favored brethren if we understand what it is to enter in and wait upon God. *I will wait for the LORD, who hid his face from the house of Jacob.*

You worship with a certain congregation, but you might not find the spiritual life or joy in the preaching or in the fellowship that you desire. You belong to a denomination with its many congregations. There may be so much error or worldliness in seeking after human wisdom and culture or trust in ordinances and observances that you are not surprised that God hides His face, and there is little power for conversion or true edification. There are also branches of Christian work with which you are connected – Sunday school, gospel hall, young men's association, or mission work abroad – in which the weakness of the Spirit's working appears to indicate that God is hiding His face. You think you know the reason. There is too much trust in men and money; there is too much formality and self-indulgence; there is too little faith and prayer; too little love and humility; too little of the Spirit of the crucified Jesus. At times you feel as if things are hopeless; nothing will help.

Believe that God can help and will help. Let the Spirit of the prophet come into you, as you value his words, and set yourself to wait on God on behalf of His erring children. Instead of the tone of judgment or condemnation, of despondency or despair, realize your calling to wait on God. If others fail to do this, double your own waiting. The deeper the darkness, the greater the need to appeal to the only Deliverer. The greater the self-confidence of those around you who don't know they are poor and wretched and blind, the more urgent the call on you who profess to see the evil and have access to Him who can help. You must be at your post waiting on God to be able to say when you are tempted to speak or to sigh, *I will wait for the LORD, who hid his face from the house of Jacob.*

There is a still larger circle – the Christian church throughout the world. Think of Greek, Roman Catholic, and Protestant churches, and the state of the millions who belong to them. Or think only of the Protestant churches with their open Bibles and orthodox creeds. How much nominal profession and formality! How much rule of the flesh and of man is found in the church of God! What abundant proof that God does hide His face!

What are we to do who see and mourn this? The first thing to be done is this: *I will wait for the LORD, who hid his face from the house of Jacob.* Let us wait on God in the humble confession of the sins of His people. Let us take time and wait on Him in this exercise. Let us wait on God in tender, loving intercession for all saints, our beloved brethren, however wrong their lives or their teaching may appear. Let us wait on God in faith and expectation, until He shows us that He will hear. Let us wait on God with the simple offering of ourselves and the earnest prayer that He will send us to our brethren. Let us wait on God and give Him no rest until He makes Zion a joy in the earth. Yes, let us rest in the Lord and wait patiently for Him who now hides His face from many of His children. And of the lifting up of the light of His countenance for which we long for all His people, let us say, *I have waited for the LORD, my soul has waited, and for his word I have waited. My soul has waited for the Lord, more than those that watch for the morning: I say, more than those that watch for the morning* (Psalm 130:5-6).

My soul, wait thou only upon God!

Eighteenth Day

Waiting to Reveal Himself

And it shall be said in that day, Behold, this
is our God, whom we have waited for, and
he has saved us: this is the LORD, whom we
have waited for, we will be glad and rejoice
in his saving health. – Isaiah 25:9

In this passage we have two precious thoughts. The one is that it is the language of God's people who have been unitedly waiting on Him; the other is that the fruit of their waiting has been that God has revealed Himself, so they could joyfully say, *Behold, this is our God, . . . this is the LORD.* The power and the blessing of united waiting is what we need to learn.

Note the twice-repeated *whom we have waited for.* In some time of trouble, the hearts of the people had been drawn together, and ceasing from all human hope or help, they had set themselves with one heart to wait for their God. Isn't this what we need in our churches and conventions and prayer meetings? Isn't the need of the church and the world great enough to demand it? Aren't there evils in the church to which no human wisdom is equal? Don't we have ritualism and rationalism, formalism and worldliness, robbing the church of its power? Don't we have culture and money and pleasure threatening its spiritual life? Aren't the powers of the church totally inadequate to cope with the powers of infidelity, iniquity, and wretchedness in Christian countries and in heathen nations? And isn't there a provision in the promise of God and in the power of the Holy Spirit that can meet the need and give the church the restful assurance that she is doing all that God expects of her? Wouldn't united waiting upon God for the supply of His Spirit be the needed blessing? We cannot doubt it.

The object of a more definite waiting upon God in our gatherings would be the same as in personal worship. It would mean a deeper conviction that God must and will do all – a more humble and abiding entrance into our deep helplessness and the need for entire and unceasing dependence upon Him. We must develop a consciousness that the essential thing is giving God His place of honor and power. This waiting upon God would bring a confident expectation that God will, by His Spirit, give the secret of His acceptance and presence, and in due time, the revelation of His saving power. The purpose would be to bring everyone in a praying and worshipping assembly under a deep sense of God's presence, so that when they part, they will have the consciousness of having met God Himself, of having left every request with Him, and of now waiting in stillness while He works out His salvation.

This experience is indicated in our text. The fulfillment of the words may be in such striking intervention of God's power that all can join in the cry, *Behold, this is our God, . . . this is the LORD.* When God's people become conscious of His presence in their waiting times, their souls may experience and with holy awe feel this declaration: *Behold, this is our God, . . . this is the LORD.* This is what is too often missed in our meetings for worship. The godly minister has no more difficult, solemn, or blessed task than to lead his people to meet God and bring each one into contact with Him before he even preaches. *Now therefore we are all here present before God* – these words of Cornelius show the way in which Peter's audience was prepared for the coming of the Holy Spirit (Acts 10:33). Waiting before God, waiting for God, and waiting on God are the one condition of God showing His presence.

An assembly of believers may gather for the one purpose of helping each other with intervals of silence to wait on God alone. They may open their hearts for whatever God might have of new discoveries of evil, of His will, of new openings in work, or of new methods of work. They would soon have reason to say, *Behold, this is our God, whom we have waited for, and he has saved us: this is the LORD, whom we have waited for, we will be glad and rejoice in His saving health.*

My soul, wait thou only upon God!

Nineteenth Day

Waiting for a God of Judgment

Yea, in the way of thy judgments, O LORD, have we waited for thee; . . . for when thy judgments are in the earth, the inhabitants of the world will learn righteousness.
– Isaiah 26:8-9 KJV

The LORD is a God of judgment: blessed are all those that wait for him. – Isaiah 30:18

Our Lord is a God of mercy and a God of judgment. Mercy and judgment are always together in His dealings. In the flood, in the deliverance of Israel out of Egypt, and in the overthrow of the Canaanites, we see mercy in the midst of judgment. In these instances with the inner circle of His own people, we see that the judgment punishes the sin, while mercy saves the sinner. Or rather, mercy saves the sinner, not in spite of, but by means of, the judgment that came upon his sin. In waiting on God, we must beware that as we wait, we can expect Him as a God of judgment.

In the way of thy judgments, O LORD, have we waited for thee. That will prove true in our inner experience. If we are honest in our longing for holiness and in our prayer to be wholly the Lord's, His holy presence will arouse and discover hidden sin and convict us of our evil nature, its opposition to God's law, and its inability to fulfill that law. The words will come true: *Who may abide the time of his coming? and who shall stand when he appears? for he shall be like a refiner's fire* (Malachi 3:2). *Oh that thou would . . . come down, . . . as when the melting fire burns* (Isaiah 64:1-2). God executes His judgments upon sin within the soul in great mercy, as He makes it feel its wickedness and guilt. Many try to flee from these judgments; the soul that longs for God and for deliverance from sin bows under them in humility and in hope. In silence the soul says, *Let God arise, let his enemies be scattered* (Psalm 68:1). *In the way of thy judgments, . . . have we waited for thee.*

Let no one who seeks to learn the blessed art of waiting on God be surprised if the attempt to wait on Him only reveals more of his own sin and darkness. Let no one despair because unconquered sins, evil thoughts, or great darkness appear to hide God's face. Wasn't that mercy hidden in His own beloved Son, the gift and bearer of His mercy on Calvary? Oh, submit and sink deep under the judgment of every sin; judgment prepares the way but releases wonderful mercy. It is written, *Zion shall be ransomed with judgment* (Isaiah 1:27). Wait on God; in the faith that His tender mercy is working out in you, His redemption is in the midst of judgment. Wait for Him, and He will be gracious to you.

There is another application – one of unspeakable solemnity. In the way of His judgments, we expect God to visit this earth; we are waiting for Him. What a thought! We know about these coming judgments; we know that tens of thousands of professing Christians live in carelessness and will perish under God's hand if they don't change. Oh, shouldn't we do our utmost to warn them and plead with and for them, so God can have mercy on them? If we understand our lack of boldness, zeal, and power, shouldn't we wait on God more definitely and persistently as a God of judgment? Shouldn't we ask Him to reveal Himself in the judgments that are coming on our friends, so that we might be inspired with a new fear of Him and for them? May we be compelled to speak and pray as never before. Truly, waiting on God is not meant to be a spiritual self-indulgence. The objective is to let God and His holiness, Christ and the love that died on Calvary, and the Spirit and fire that burns in heaven and came to earth, get possession of us to warn and rouse men with the message that we are waiting for God and His judgments. O Christian, prove that you really believe in the God of judgment.

My soul, wait thou only upon God!

Twentieth Day

God Who Waits on Us

And therefore will the LORD wait for you,
that he may have mercy on you, and therefore
will he be exalted having mercy upon you: for
the LORD is a God of judgment: blessed are
all those that wait for him. – Isaiah 30:18

We must not only think of our waiting upon
God, but also of God's waiting upon us. The
vision of Him waiting on us will give new passion
and inspiration to our waiting on Him. It will give
an unspeakable confidence that our waiting is not in
vain. If He waits for us, then we can be sure that we are
more than welcome and that He rejoices to find those
He has been seeking.

Let us seek at this moment, in the spirit of humbly
waiting on God, to discover something of what it
means. *Therefore will the LORD wait for you, that he*
may have mercy on you. We shall accept and echo back
the message: *Blessed are all those that wait for him.*

Look up and see the great God upon His throne. He is love – an unceasing and inexpressible desire to communicate His own goodness and blessedness to all His creatures. He longs and delights to bless. He has inconceivably glorious purposes for every one of His children to reveal His love and power in them by the power of His Holy Spirit. He waits with all the longings of a father's heart. He waits that He may be gracious unto you. And each time you wait upon Him or seek to maintain the habit of waiting in daily life, you may look up and see Him ready to meet you and be gracious unto you. Yes, connect every exercise and every breath of the waiting life with faith's vision of your God waiting for you.

But if He waits to be gracious even after I come and wait upon Him, why doesn't He give the help I seek, but rather waits longer and longer? One reason is this: God is a wise husbandman who *waiteth for the precious fruit of the earth, and hath long patience for it* (James 5:7 KJV). He cannot gather the fruit until it is ripe. He knows when we are spiritually ready to receive the blessing to our profit and His glory. Waiting in the sunshine of His love is what will ripen the soul for His blessing. Waiting under the cloud of trial that breaks in showers of blessing is as needful. Be assured that if God waits longer than you want, it is only to make the blessing doubly precious. God waited four thousand years before He sent His Son; our times are in His hands. He will avenge His elect speedily; He will hurry to help and not delay one hour too long.

The other reason He waits points to what has been

said before. The giver is more than the gift; God is more than the blessing; and our waiting on Him is the only way to learn to find our life and joy in Him. Oh, if God's children only knew what a glorious God they have and what a privilege it is to be linked in fellowship with Him, then they would rejoice in Him, and even when He keeps them waiting, they would learn to understand better than ever. *Therefore will the LORD wait for you, that he may have mercy on you.* His waiting will be the highest proof of His graciousness. *Blessed are all those that wait for him.*

The queen has her ladies-in-waiting, or attendants. The position is one of subordination and service, but it is considered a position of the highest dignity and privilege, because a wise and gracious sovereign makes them companions and friends. What a dignity and blessedness to be attendants-in-waiting on the everlasting God, always on the watch for every indication of His will or favor and always conscious of His nearness, His goodness, and His grace. *The LORD is good unto those that wait in him* (Lamentations 3:25). *Blessed are all those that wait for him.* What a blessing when a waiting soul and a waiting God meet each other! God cannot do His work without His waiting and our waiting for His time; let waiting be our work, as it is His. And if His waiting is nothing but goodness and graciousness, let ours be nothing but a rejoicing in that goodness and a confident expectancy of that grace. Let every thought of waiting become simply the expression of unmingled and unutterable blessedness, because it brings us to a

God who waits so that He may make Himself known to us perfectly as the Gracious One.

My soul, wait thou only upon God!

Twenty-First Day

The Almighty One

Those that wait for the LORD shall have new strength; they shall mount up with wings as eagles; they shall run and not be weary; and they shall walk, and not faint. – Isaiah 40:31

Waiting always involves the character of our thoughts of the one on whom we wait. Our waiting on God will depend on our faith in what He is. In our text we have the close of a passage in which God reveals Himself as the everlasting and almighty One. It is as that revelation enters our soul that the waiting becomes the spontaneous expression of what we know Him to be – a God altogether worthy to be waited upon.

Listen to the words: *Why sayest thou, O Jacob, and speakest thou, O Israel, My way is hid from the LORD* (Isaiah 40:27). Why do you speak as if God does not hear or help?

Hast thou not known? Hast thou not heard that the

God of the age is the LORD, the Creator of the ends of the earth? He does not faint, nor is he weary (Isaiah 40:28). Far from it, for *He gives power to the faint; and to those that have no might he increases strength* (Isaiah 40:29). *The glory of young men is their strength,* but *the young men faint and are weary; the children stumble and fall* (Proverbs 20:29; Isaiah 40:30). All that is considered strong with man shall come to nothing. *Those that wait for the LORD shall have new strength; they shall mount up with wings as eagles; they shall run and not be weary; and they shall walk, and not faint* (Isaiah 40:31). They shall be strong with the strength of God, *and they shall walk, and not faint.*

Yes, *they shall mount up with wings as eagles.* What does *wings as eagles* mean? The eagle is the king of birds; it soars the highest into the heavens. Believers are to live a heavenly life in the very presence and love and joy of God. They are to live where God lives; they need God's strength to rise to that height. To them that wait on Him it shall be given.

How are these eagles' wings obtained? Only in one way – by the eagle birth. You are born of God, so you have the eagles' wings. You may not have known it, and you may not have used them, but God can and will teach you to use them.

You know how the eagles are taught the use of their wings. Watch the distant cliff that rises a thousand feet out of the sea. High on a ledge on the rock is an eagle's nest with its treasure of two young eaglets. See the mother bird come, stir up her nest, and with her beak push the timid birds over the precipice. See how they flutter and fall and sink toward the depth. But the mother eagle *flutters over her young, spreads abroad her wings, takes them, bears them on her wings* (Deuteronomy 32:11). They ride on her wings, and she brings them to a place of safety. She does this over and over, each time casting them out over the precipice and then catching and carrying them. *So the LORD alone did lead him* (Deuteronomy 32:12). Yes, the instinct of that mother eagle was God's gift, a single ray of that love in which the Almighty trains His people to mount as on eagles' wings.

He stirs up your nest. He disappoints your hopes. He brings down your confidence. He makes you fear and tremble, as all your strength fails, and you feel utterly weary and helpless. And all the while, He spreads His strong wings for you to rest your weakness on and offers His everlasting Creator strength to work in you. All He asks is that you sink down in your weariness, wait on Him, and allow Him in His Jehovah strength to carry you as you ride on the wings of His omnipotence.

Dear child of God, I pray you lift up your eyes and behold your God. Listen to Him who said He does not faint or grow weary; He promises that you too will not faint or be weary and asks nothing except this – that you wait on Him. Let your answer be – with such a God, so mighty, so faithful, so tender:

My soul, wait thou only upon God!

Twenty-Second Day

The Certainty of Blessing

Thou shalt know that I am the LORD: for those that wait for me shall not be ashamed.
– Isaiah 49:23

Blessed are all those that wait for him.
– Isaiah 30:18

What promises! How God seeks to draw us to wait on Him with the most positive assurance that it will never be in vain: *Those that wait for me shall not be ashamed*. Though we have often experienced this, we are still slow to learn that this blessed waiting must and can be the very breath of our life. It is a continuous resting in God's presence and His love and an unceasing submission to Him to perfect His work in us. Listen and meditate, until our hearts can say with new conviction: *Blessed are all those that wait for him*. In the prayer of Psalm 25 we read, *Let me not be ashamed* (verses 2 and 20). The very prayer shows how we fear that it might not be so. Let us listen to God's answer until every fear is banished, and we send back to heaven the words God speaks. Yes, Lord, we believe what You say: *those that wait for me shall not be ashamed* (Isaiah 49:23). *Blessed are all those that wait for him* (Isaiah 30:18).

The context of these two passages points us to times when God's church was in trouble, and to the human eye there seemed to be no possibilities of deliverance. But God interjects with His word of promise and pledges His almighty power for the deliverance of His people. As the God who has undertaken the work of their redemption, He invites them to wait on Him and assures them that disappointment is impossible. We too are living in days when much in the state of the church with its profession and formalism is indescribably sad. Amid all we praise God for, there is much to mourn over. If it wasn't for God's promises, we might despair. But in His promises, the living God has given and bound Himself to us. He calls us to wait on Him. He assures us that we shall not be put to shame. Oh, that our hearts might learn to wait before Him, until He reveals what His promises mean to us, and in the promises He reveals Himself in His hidden glory. We shall be drawn to wait on Him alone. May God increase the company of those who say, *Our soul waited for the LORD; he is our help and our shield* (Psalm 33:20).

This waiting upon God on behalf of His church and people will depend greatly upon the place that waiting on Him has taken in our personal life. The mind may often have beautiful visions of what God has promised to do, and the lips may speak of them in stirring words, but these are not the measure of our faith or power. No, it is what we know of God in our personal experience, as He conquers the enemies within, as He reigns, rules, and reveals Himself in His holiness and power in our inmost being. That is the real measure of the spiritual blessing we expect from Him, and that we can bring to our fellow men. As we know how blessed the waiting on God has become to our own souls, we shall confidently hope in the blessing to come on the church around us. The key word of all our expectations will be *for those that wait for me shall not be ashamed.* From what He has done in us, we shall trust Him to do mighty things around us.

Blessed are all those that wait for him. Yes, blessed even now in the waiting. The promised blessings for us or for others may tarry, but the unutterable blessedness of knowing and having Him, the divine blesser and the living fountain of the coming blessings, is ours even now. Allow this truth to possess your souls, so that waiting on God is the highest privilege of the creature, the highest blessedness of His redeemed child.

Even as the sunshine enters with its light and warmth and its beauty and blessing into every little blade of grass that rises upward out of the cold earth, so the everlasting God meets each waiting child in the greatness and the tenderness of His love. He shines *in our hearts to bring forth the light of the knowledge of the clarity* [glory] *of God in the face of Jesus Christ* (2 Corinthians 4:6).

Read these words again until your heart learns to know what God waits to do in you. Who can measure the difference between the great sun and that little blade of grass? Still, the grass has all of the sun it can need or hold. Do believe that in waiting on God, His greatness and your littleness meet and suit each other wonderfully. Do you see how in emptiness, poverty, and utter impotence, in humility, meekness, and surrender to His will, you can be still? As you wait on Him, God draws nigh. He will reveal Himself as the God who will fulfill mightily His every promise. Let your heart always take up the song: *Blessed are all those that wait for him.*

My soul, wait thou only upon God!

Waiting for Unexpected Things

For since the beginning of the world men have not heard, nor perceived by the ear, neither hath the eye seen, O God, beside thee, what he hath prepared for him that waiteth for him. – Isaiah 64:4 KJV

The American Standard Version says, *Neither hath the eye seen a God besides thee, who worketh for him that waiteth for him.* In the King James Version, the thought is that no eye has seen *what* God has prepared. In both versions, the two thoughts are common: our place is to wait upon God, and what the human heart cannot conceive will be revealed to us. The difference is that in the ASV it is the God who works, and in the KJV no eye has seen what He has prepared for man to work. In 1 Corinthians 2, the citation is in regard to the things which the Holy Spirit will reveal, as in the KJV above, and that is the view we will take in this meditation.

The previous verses in Isaiah, especially from Isaiah 63:15, refer to the low state of God's people. The prayer has been poured out, *Look down from heaven* (Isaiah 63:15). *Hast thou hardened our heart to thy fear? Return for thy slaves* (Isaiah 63:17). And even more urgent: *Oh that thou would rend the heavens, that thou would come down, . . . as when the melting fire burns, . . . to make thy name known to thine adversaries* (Isaiah 64:1-2). Then follows the plea from the past: *when thou didst terrible things which we did not look for, that the mountains flowed down at thy presence* (Isaiah 64:3). This is now the faith that has been awakened by the thought of things we did not look for; He is still the same God. *Neither hath the eye hath seen, O God, beside thee, what he hath prepared for him that waiteth for him.* God alone knows what He can do for His waiting people. As Paul expounds and applies this, he says, *No one has known the things of God, but the Spirit of God* (1 Corinthians 2:11). *But God has revealed this unto us by His Spirit* (1 Corinthians 2:10).

The need of God's people and the call for God's intervention is as urgent in our days as it was in the time of Isaiah. There is now, as there was then, as there has been at all times, a remnant that seeks after God with their whole heart. But if we look at Christendom as a whole, at the state of the church of Christ, we have infinite cause for begging God to part the heavens and come down. Nothing but a special intervention of almighty power will help us. I fear we have no idea of what the so-called Christian world should be in the sight of God. Unless God comes as when the melting fire burns to make His name known to His adversaries, our labors are equally fruitless. Look at the ministry – how much of it is in the wisdom of man and of literary culture. How little is the demonstration of the Spirit and of power. Think of the unity of the body – how little is the manifestation of the power of a heavenly love that binds God's children into one. Think of holiness, the holiness of Christlike humility and crucifixion to the world – how little the world sees that they have men among them who live in Christ and in whom Christ and heaven live.

What is to be done? There is only one thing. We must wait upon God. And what for? We must cry with a cry that never rests, *Oh that thou would rend the heavens, that thou would come down, that the mountains might flow down at thy presence*. We must desire and believe; we must ask and expect that God will do unlooked-for things. We must set our faith on a God of whom men do not know what He has prepared for them who wait for Him. The wonder-doing God, who can surpass all our expectations, must be the God of our confidence.

Yes, let God's people enlarge their hearts to wait on a God able to do exceeding abundantly above what we can ask or think (Ephesians 3:20). Let us band together as His elect who cry day and night to Him for things men have not seen. He is able to arise and make His people a name and a praise in the earth. *And therefore will the LORD wait for you, that he may have mercy on you, . . . blessed are all those that wait for him.*

My soul, wait thou only upon God!

Waiting to Know His Goodness

The LORD is good unto those that wait in him. – Lamentations 3:25

There is none good but one, that is, God (Matthew 19:17). His goodness is in the heavens. *Oh how great is thy goodness, which thou hast laid up for those that fear thee* (Psalm 31:19). *O taste and see that the LORD is good* (Psalm 34:8). And, the true way of entering into and rejoicing in this goodness of God is by waiting upon Him. The Lord is good, but His children often do not know it, and they don't wait in quietness for Him to reveal it. But to those who persevere in waiting, whose souls do wait, it will come true. One might think that only those who have to wait might be the doubters. But this is only when they grow impatient. The truly waiting ones will all say, *The LORD is good unto those that wait in him.* If you desire to fully know the goodness of God, give yourself more than ever to a life of waiting on Him.

As we first start waiting upon God, our heart is chiefly set upon receiving the blessings. God graciously uses our need and desire for help to educate us for something higher than we imagine. We seek gifts; He, the Giver, longs to give Himself and satisfy our soul with His goodness. For this reason He often withholds the gifts, and the time of waiting is prolonged. He continually seeks to win the heart of His child for Himself. He wishes that when He bestows the gift, we would say how good God is even when it takes a long time to come or if it never comes. We should always be experiencing this: *It is good to wait quietly* (Lamentations 3:26). *The LORD is good unto those that wait in him.*

What a blessed life the life of waiting then becomes with the continual worship of faith, as we adore and trust His goodness. As the soul learns this secret, every act or exercise of waiting becomes a quiet entering into the goodness of God to let it do its blessed work and satisfy our every need. And every experience of God's goodness gives the work of waiting new attractiveness; instead of only taking refuge in time of need, we acquire a great longing to wait continually throughout the day. Whatever duties and engagements occupy our time and mind, the soul becomes more familiar with the secret art of always waiting. Waiting becomes our habit and disposition; it becomes second nature and the breath of our soul.

Dear Christian, don't you see that waiting is not one among a number of Christian virtues to be thought of from time to time, but it expresses the disposition that lies at the very root of the Christian life? It gives a higher value and a new power to our prayer and worship, to our faith and surrender, because it links us in unalterable dependence on God Himself. And it gives us the unbroken enjoyment of the goodness of God: *The LORD is good unto those that wait in him.*

Take time and trouble to cultivate this waiting that is so needed in the Christian life. We get too much religion secondhand from the teaching of men. That teaching has great value if it leads us to God Himself, even as the preaching of John the Baptist sent his disciples away from himself to the living Christ.

What our religion needs is more of God. Many of us are too occupied with our work. As with Martha, the very service we want to render for the Master separates us from Him; it is neither pleasing to Him nor profitable to ourselves. The more we work, the more we need to wait upon God; the doing of God's will would then be our meat and drink, our nourishment and refreshment and strength, instead of a means of exhausting us. *The LORD is good unto those that wait in him.* How good none can tell except those who prove it in waiting on Him. How good none can fully tell except those who have proved Him to the utmost.

My soul, wait thou only upon God!

Waiting Quietly

It is good to wait quietly for the salvation in the LORD. – Lamentations 3:26

Take heed, and be quiet; do not fear, neither be fainthearted (Isaiah 7:4). *In quietness and in confidence shall be your strength* (Isaiah 30:15). Such words reveal the close connection between quietness and faith, and they show us what a deep need there is for quietness as a component of true waiting on God. If we are to have our whole heart turned towards God, we must have it turned away from the creature, from all that occupies and interests, whether from joy or sorrow.

God is a Being of infinite greatness and glory, and our nature has become so estranged from Him that it needs our whole heart and all our desires set upon Him even in some little measure to know and receive Him. Everything that is not of God that excites our fears, stirs our efforts, awakens our hopes, or makes us glad hinders us in our perfect waiting on Him. The message is one of deep meaning: *Take heed, and be quiet. In quietness . . . shall be your strength. It is good to wait quietly.*

The very thought of God in His majesty and holiness should silence us. Scripture abundantly testifies:

> *The LORD is in his holy temple: let all the earth keep silence before him.* (Habakkuk 2:20)

> *Be silent before the presence of the Lord GOD.* (Zephaniah 1:7)

> *Be silent, O all flesh, before the LORD, for he is raised up out of his holy habitation.* (Zechariah 2:13)

As long as the waiting on God is chiefly regarded as an end towards more effectual prayer and the obtaining of our petitions, this spirit of perfect quietness will not be obtained. But when the waiting on God is seen as an unspeakable blessedness and one of the highest forms of fellowship with the Holy One, the adoration of Him in His glory will humble the soul into a holy stillness and make way for God to speak and reveal Himself. Then the fulfillment of the precious promise that all of self and self-effort will be humbled comes: *The lofty looks of man shall be humbled, . . . and the LORD alone shall be exalted in that day* (Isaiah 2:11).

Let everyone who desires to learn the art of waiting on God remember the lesson: *Take heed, and be quiet. It is good to wait quietly.* Take time to be separate from all friends and all duties, all cares and all joys; take time to be still and quiet before God. Take time to secure stillness not only from man and the world, but also from self and your energy. Let the Word and prayer be precious; but remember, even these may hinder the quiet waiting. The activity of the mind in studying the Word or expressing its thoughts in prayer, and the activities of the heart with its desires and hopes and fears may engage us so much that we do not come to the still waiting on the all-glorious One. Our whole being needs to be bowed low in silence before Him. At first it may seem difficult to know how to wait quietly with the activities of mind and heart subdued, but every effort will be rewarded. We will find that quiet waiting becomes pleasant, and the little time of silent worship will bring a peace and a rest that give a blessing not only in prayer, but also all day long.

It is good to wait quietly for the salvation in the LORD. Yes, it is good. The quietness is the confession of our helplessness. With all our willing and running, with all our thinking and praying, quiet waiting will not be done; we must receive it from God. Quietness is the confession of our trust that our God will in His time come to our help – the quiet resting in Him alone. It is the confession of our desire to sink into our nothingness and to let Him work and reveal Himself. Let us wait quietly. Let there be a quiet reverence, an abiding watchfulness against our connection with the world in our soul that waits for God to do His wondrous work in our daily lives. May our whole character come to bear the beautiful countenance: quietly waiting for the salvation of God.

My soul, wait thou only upon God!

Twenty-Sixth Day

Waiting in Holy Expectancy

Therefore I will wait for the LORD; I will wait for the God of my saving health [salvation]; *my God will hear me.* – Micah 7:7

Have you ever read a beautiful little book, *Expectation Corner*? If not, you should get a copy; you will find in it one of the best sermons on our text. It tells of a king who prepared a city for some of his poor subjects. Not far from them were large storehouses, where everything they could need was supplied if they just sent in their requests. But there was one condition – they were to watch for the answer, so that when the king's messengers came with the answer to their petitions, they would always be found waiting and ready to receive them. The sad story is told of one despondent person who never expected to get what he requested, because he believed he was too unworthy. One day he was taken to the king's storehouses, and to his amazement, he saw all the packages that had been made up for him with his address and sent. There was the garment of praise, the oil of joy, the eye salve, and so much more. The messengers had been to his door but found it closed; he was not watching. From that time on, he learned the lesson that Micah taught. *I will wait for the LORD; I will wait for the God of my saving health; my God will hear me.*

Waiting for the answer to prayer is only part of waiting. We want to realize the blessed truth that waiting is only a part – but a very important part. When we have special petitions in connection with what we are waiting for, our waiting must be the confident assurance of *my God will hear me.* A holy, joyful expectancy is the very essence of true waiting. This is not only in reference to the many requests every believer makes, but also to the one petition that should be chief in every heart – that the life of God in the soul may have full charge. That Christ may be fully formed within us and that we may be filled to all the fullness of God is what God has promised. God's people too seldom seek this – often because they do not believe it is possible. This is what we ought to seek and dare to expect, because God is able and waiting to work it in us.

But God Himself must work it, and therefore our working must cease. We must see how the faith of the power of God who raised Jesus from the dead as well as the resurrection and the perfecting of God's life in our souls is to be directly His work. Waiting must become more than a tarrying before God in the stillness of our soul and counting on Him who raises the dead.

Notice how the threefold use of the name of God

in our text points us to Him as the one from whom is our expectation. *I will wait for the LORD. I will wait for the God of my saving health. My God will hear me.* Everything that pertains to salvation and everything that is good and holy must be the direct, mighty work of God Himself within us. Every moment of a life in the will of God must be the immediate operation of God. And the one thing I have to do is look to the Lord, to wait for the God of my salvation, and to hold fast with confident assurance that *my God will hear me.*

God says, *Be still, and know that I am God.* There is no stillness like that of the grave. In the grave of Jesus, in the fellowship of His death, in death to self with its will and wisdom, its strength and energy, there is rest. As we cease from self and our soul becomes still to God, God will arise and show Himself. *Be still, and know* – then you shall know – *that I am God.* There is no stillness like the stillness Jesus gives when He speaks: *Peace, be still* (Mark 4:39). In Christ, in His death, in His life, and in His perfected redemption, the soul may be still, and God will come in, take possession, and do His perfect work.

My soul, wait thou only upon God!

Twenty-Seventh Day

Waiting for Redemption

Simeon, . . . was just and devout, waiting
for the consolation of Israel, and the Holy
Spirit was upon him. . . . Anna, a prophetess,
. . . spoke of him to all those that looked for
redemption in Jerusalem. – Luke 2:25, 36, 38

H ere we have the mark of a waiting believer. *Just*
– righteous in all his conduct; *devout* – devoted
to God, always walking as in His presence; *waiting for*
the consolation of Israel – looking for the fulfillment
of God's promises; *and the Holy Spirit was upon him.*
In the devout waiting, he had been prepared for the
blessing. And Simeon was not the only one. Anna
spoke of him to all those that looked for redemption in
Jerusalem. This was the one mark amid surrounding
formalism and worldliness of a godly band of men and
women in Jerusalem. They were waiting on God and
looking for His promised redemption.

Now that the consolation of Israel has come, and

the redemption has been accomplished, do we still need to wait? We do indeed, but won't our waiting differ greatly from those who looked forward to it as coming? It will, particularly in two respects. We now wait on God in the full power of the redemption, and we wait for its full revelation.

Our waiting is in the full power of the redemption. Christ spoke, *At that day ye shall know that I am in my Father, and ye in me* (John 14:20). Abide in Me? The Epistles teach us to present ourselves to God as *dead unto sin, but alive unto God in Christ, Jesus, our Lord*, and that we are blessed *with all spiritual blessings in heavenly things in Christ* (Romans 6:11; Ephesians 1:3). Our waiting on God may now be in the wonderful consciousness, wrought and maintained by the Holy Spirit within us, that we are accepted in the Beloved, that the love that rests on Him rests on us, and that we are living in that love in the very nearness, presence, and sight of God. The old saints took their stand on the Word of God; waiting and hoping on that Word, we can rest on the Word too. But oh, as one with Christ Jesus, we have exceedingly greater privileges. In our waiting on God, let this be our confidence: in Christ we have access to the Father, so we may be sure that our waiting is not in vain.

Our waiting also differs in that while they waited for a redemption to come, we see it accomplished and now wait for its revelation in us. Christ not only said, *Abide in me*, but also, *I in you* (John 15:4). The Epistles not only speak of us *in Christ* but also of Christ *in us*, as the highest mystery of redeeming love (Colossians 1:27). As we maintain our place in Christ day by day, God waits to reveal Christ in us in such a way that He is formed in us, and His mind and disposition and likeness acquire form and substance in us, so that each believer can in truth say, *Christ lives in me* (Galatians 2:20).

My life in Christ up there in heaven and Christ's life in me down here on earth complement each other. The more my waiting on God is marked by the living faith *in Christ*, the more my heart thirsts for and claims the Christ in me. And the waiting on God, which began with special needs and prayer, will be concentrated on one thing – Lord, reveal Your redemption fully in me; let Christ live in me.

Our waiting differs from that of the old saints in the place we take and the expectations we entertain. But it is essentially the same: waiting on God – from whom alone is our expectation.

Learn one lesson from Simeon and Anna. How utterly impossible it was for them to do anything towards the great redemption – towards the birth of Christ or His death. It was God's work. They could do nothing but wait. Are we as helpless in regard to the revelation of Christ in us? We are indeed. God did not work out the great redemption in Christ and leave its application in detail to us.

The secret thought that it is so, lies at the root of all our weakness. The revelation of Christ in every individual believer and the daily revelation in each one, step by step and moment by moment, is as much the work of God's omnipotence as the birth or resurrection of Christ. Until this truth enters and fills us, and we feel that we are just as dependent upon God for each moment of our life in the enjoyment of redemption as Simeon and Anna were in their waiting for it, our waiting upon God will not bring its full blessing. The sense of utter and absolute helplessness and the confidence that God can and will do all must be the marks of our waiting as much as theirs was. As gloriously as God proved Himself to be the faithful and wonder-working God to them, He will do so to us also.

My soul, wait thou only upon God!

Twenty-Eighth Day

Waiting for the Coming of His Son

And ye yourselves like unto men that wait for their lord. – Luke 12:36

Until the appearing of our Lord Jesus Christ, who in his time shall show the blessed and only Potentate, the King of kings, and Lord of lords. – 1 Timothy 6:14-15

Converted to God from idols to serve the living and true God and to wait for his Son from the heavens. – 1 Thessalonians 1:9-10

God has joined the waiting on God in heaven and waiting for His Son from heaven, and no man can separate them. The waiting on God for His presence and power in daily life will be the only true preparation for waiting for Christ in humility and true holiness. The waiting for Christ coming from heaven to take us to heaven will give the waiting on God its true tone of hopefulness and joy. The Father who will reveal His Son from heaven in His own time is the God who prepares us for the revelation of His Son as we wait. The present life and the coming glory are inseparably connected in God and in us.

There is sometimes a danger of separating them. It is always easier to be engaged with the religion of the past or the future than to be faithful in the religion of today. As we look at what God has done in the past or will do in time to come, the personal claim of present duty and present submission to His working may be downplayed. Waiting on God must lead to waiting for Christ as the glorious consummation of His work; waiting for Christ must remind us of the duty of waiting upon God as our only proof that the waiting for Christ is in spirit and in truth.

There is a danger of being more occupied with the things to come than with the One who is to come. And, the study of future events is so extensive for imagination, reason, and human ingenuity that only humble waiting on God can save us from mistaking the interest and pleasure of intellectual study for the true love of Him and His appearing.

If you say you wait for Christ's coming, be sure that you wait on God now. All you who seek to wait on God to reveal His Son in you, see to it that you do so as men waiting for the revelation of His Son from heaven. The hope of that glorious appearing will strengthen you while you wait for what He will do in you now. The same omnipotent love that will reveal that glory is working in you even now to fit you for it.

That blessed hope and the glorious appearing of our great God and Saviour Jesus Christ is one of the great bonds of union given to God's church throughout the ages (Titus 2:13). *He shall come to be glorified in his saints and to be admired in all those that believe* (2 Thessalonians 1:10). Then we shall all meet, and the unity of the body of Christ will be seen in its divine glory. It will be the meeting place and the triumph of divine love.

Jesus will receive His own and present them to the Father. His own will meet Him and worship that blessed face in speechless love. His own will meet each other in the ecstasy of God's own love. Let us wait, long for, and love the appearing of our Lord and heavenly Bridegroom. Tender love for Him and tender love for each other is the true and only bridal spirit. I fear that this is sometimes forgotten.

A beloved brother in Holland spoke about the expectancy of faith being the true sign of the bride. I ventured to express a doubt. An unworthy bride about to be married to a prince might only be thinking of the position and the riches that she is to receive. The expectancy of faith might be strong, and true love completely lacking. It is not when we are most occupied with prophetic subjects, but when in humility and love we are clinging close to our Lord and His brethren that we are in the bride's place. Jesus refuses to accept our love except as it is love for His disciples. Waiting for His coming means waiting for the glorious coming manifestation of the unity in the body, while we seek to maintain that unity in humility and love. Those who love most are the most ready for His coming. Love for each other is the life and beauty of His bride, the church.

And how is this to be brought about? Beloved child of God, if you want to learn to wait for His Son from heaven, live even now waiting on God in heaven. Remember how Jesus always waited on God. He could do nothing by Himself. God perfected His Son through suffering and then exalted Him. God alone can give you the deep spiritual life of one who is waiting for His Son. Wait on God for it. Waiting for Christ Himself is so different from waiting for things that may come to pass. Any Christian can wait for future events, but God must work in you every day by His Holy Spirit to wait for Christ. Therefore, all who wait on God look to Him for grace to wait for His Son to come from heaven in the Spirit. And you who want to wait for His Son must wait on God continually to reveal Christ in you.

The revelation of Christ in us as it is given to them who wait upon God is the true preparation for the full revelation of Christ in glory.

My soul, wait thou only upon God!

Twenty-Ninth Day

Waiting for the Promise of the Father

He commanded them that they should not depart from Jerusalem, but wait for the promise of the Father. – Acts 1:4

In speaking of Simeon and Anna and the saints in Jerusalem at Christ's birth, we saw how the call to wait is no less urgent now than it was then, even though the redemption they waited for has come. We wait for the full revelation in us of what came to them but what they could scarcely comprehend. In one sense, the fulfillment can never come again as it came at Pentecost. In another sense, we daily need to wait for the Father to fulfill His promise in us – in as deep a reality as with the first disciples.

The Holy Spirit is not a person distinct from the Father in the way two persons on earth are distinct. The Father and the Spirit are never without or separate from each other. The Father is always in the Spirit; the Spirit works nothing but as the Father works in Him. Each moment the same Spirit that is in us is in God too, and he who is most full of the Spirit will be the first to wait on God most earnestly to fulfill His promise and strengthen him mightily by His Spirit in the inner man. The Spirit in us is not a power at our disposal. Nor is the Spirit an independent power, acting apart from the Father and the Son. The Spirit is the real, living presence and the power of the Father working in us. Therefore, he who knows that the Spirit is in him waits on the Father for the full revelation and experience of the Spirit's indwelling with His increase and abounding more and more.

We see this in the apostles. They were filled with the Spirit at Pentecost. When they returned from the council where they had been forbidden to preach, they prayed for boldness to speak in His name, for a fresh coming of the Holy Spirit was the Father's fulfillment of His promise.

At Samaria, many had been converted by the Word, and the whole city filled with joy. At the apostles' prayer, the Father once again fulfilled the promise of the Holy Spirit. Likewise, when speaking of the waiting company in his house, Cornelius said to Peter, *We are all here present before God* (Acts 10:33). Also, in Acts 13, it was when men prayed and fasted that the promise of the Father was fulfilled, and the Spirit said, *Separate me Barnabas and Saul for the work unto which I have called them* (Acts 13:2).

In Ephesians we also find Paul praying for those who

had been sealed with the Spirit, that God would grant them the spirit of illumination (Ephesians 1:18). And later Paul prayed that God would grant them *according to the riches of his glory, to be strengthened with might by his Spirit in the inner man* (Ephesians 3:16).

The Spirit given at Pentecost was not a being that failed God in heaven, so that God sent Him out of heaven to earth. God does not, He cannot, give anything in that way. When He gives grace, or strength, or life, He gives it by giving Himself to work it; it is all inseparable from Him.[1] And, it is even more inseparable from the Holy Spirit. He is God, present and working in us – the true position that we can count on with an unceasing power as we praise Him for what we have and wait for the Father's promise to be more mightily fulfilled.

What new meaning and promise does this give to our life of waiting! It teaches us to keep the place where the disciples tarried at the footstool of the throne. It reminds us that as helpless as they were to meet their enemies or to preach to Christ's enemies before they received power, so we too need that power. We can only be strong in the life of faith or the work of love as we are in direct communication with God and Christ, with the life of the Spirit in us. It assures us that the omnipotent God will work a power in us through the glorified Christ that can bring to pass unexpected and impossible things. Oh, what won't the church be able to do when her individual members learn to live their lives by waiting on God. With all of self and the world sacrificed in the fire of love, they will unite in waiting

1   See endnote on William Law, *The Power of the Spirit*.

with one accord for the promise of the Father, once so gloriously fulfilled but still unexhausted.

Come and let each of us be still in the presence of the inconceivable grandeur of this prospect – the Father is waiting to fill the church with the Holy Spirit. Let each of us say, "He is willing to fill me."

With this faith may a hush and a holy fear come over the soul, as it waits in stillness to receive all. Let life become a deep joy in the hope of the fulfillment of the Father's promise.

My soul, wait thou only upon God!

Thirtieth Day

Waiting Continually

*Therefore be thou converted unto thy God;
keep mercy and judgment, and in thy God
wait continually.* – Hosea 12:6

Continuity is one of the essential elements of life.
Interrupt it for a single hour in a man, and it is
lost; he is dead. Unbroken and ceaseless continuity
is essential to a healthy Christian life. God wants
me to be, God waits to make me, I want to be, and I
wait on Him to make me what He expects of me and
what is pleasing in His sight. If waiting on God is the
essence of true religion, the maintenance of the spirit
of entire dependence must be continuous. The call of
God, *in thy God wait continually*, must be accepted
and obeyed. There may be times of special waiting
when the disposition and habit of soul must be there
unchanging and uninterrupted.

This waiting continually is indeed a necessity. To
those who are content with a feeble Christian life, waiting appears to be a luxury beyond what is essential for

a good Christian. But some are praying, "Lord, make me as holy as a pardoned sinner can be made. Keep me as near to You as it is possible for me to be. Fill me as full of Your love as You are willing to." Those who are praying these prayers feel that there can be no unbroken fellowship with God, no full abiding in Christ, and no constant victory over sin and readiness for service without waiting continually on the Lord.

Continual waiting is a possibility. Many think that it is out of the question with the duties of life. They cannot be thinking of it all the time. Even when they wish to, they forget.

They do not understand that it is a matter of the heart, and what the heart is full of occupies it, even when the thoughts are otherwise engaged. A father's heart may be filled continuously with intense love and longing for a sick wife or child from a distance, even though pressing business requires all his thoughts.

When the heart has learned how powerless it is to keep itself or bring forth any good, when it has learned how surely and truly God will keep it, and when it has accepted God's promise to do the impossible for it, it learns to rest in God. In the midst of occupations and temptations, it can wait continually.

This waiting is a promise. God's commands are enablings; gospel precepts are all promises, a revelation of what our God will do for us. When you begin to wait on God, it is with frequent intermission and frequent failure, but God is watching over you in love and secretly strengthening you in it. Sometimes waiting appears to be lost time, but it is not. Waiting, even in darkness, is unconscious progress, because it is God you have to work with, and He is working in you. God who calls you to wait on Him sees your feeble efforts and works it in you. Your spiritual life is in no respect your own work. As little as you begin the work of waiting, can you continue it? God's Spirit is the One who has begun the work in you of waiting upon God; He will enable you to wait continually.

Waiting continually will be met and rewarded by God working continually. We are coming to the end of our meditations. If only you and I might learn one lesson: God must and God will work continually. He does work continually, but the experience of His work is hindered by unbelief. He who by His Spirit teaches you to wait continually will bring you to experience how His work is never ceasing. In the love and the life and the work of God, there can be no break or interruption.

Do not limit God by your thoughts of what might be expected. Fix your eyes upon this one truth: in His very nature, God, as the only Giver of life, cannot do otherwise than to work in His child. Don't just look at the one side: if I wait continually, God will work continually. No, look at the other side. Place God first and say, "God works continually, so every moment I may wait on Him – continually." Take time until the vision of your God working continually without one moment's interruption fills your being. Your waiting continually will then come by itself. The holy habit of the soul will be full of trust and joy. *I have waited for thee all the day.* The Holy Spirit will keep you waiting.

My soul, wait thou only upon God!

Moment By Moment[2]

I the LORD do keep it; I will water it every moment. (Isaiah 27:3)

Dying with Jesus, by death reckoned mine,
Living with Jesus a new life divine;
Looking to Jesus till glory doth shine,
Moment by moment, O Lord, I am Thine.

Chorus – Moment by moment I'm kept in His love,
Moment by moment I've life from above;
Looking to Jesus till glory doth shine;
Moment by moment, O Lord, I am Thine,

Never a battle with wrong for the right,
Never a contest that He doth not fight;
Lifting above us His banner so white,
Moment by moment I'm kept in His sight.

---

2   Daniel W. Whittle, *Christian Endeavour Hymns*, ed. Ira D. Sankey (New York: United Society of Christian Endeavor, 1894), 88.

Chorus.

Never a trial that He is not there,
Never a burden that He doth not bear,
Never a sorrow that He doth not share,
Moment by moment I'm under His care.

Chorus.

Never a heartache, and never a groan,
Never a teardrop, and never a moan;
Never a danger but there on the throne
Moment by moment He thinks of His own.

Chorus.

Never a weakness that He doth not feel,
Never a sickness that He cannot heal;
Moment by moment, in woe or in weal,
Jesus, my Savior, abides with me still.

Thirty-First Day

Only Waiting

My soul, wait thou only upon God; for my
expectation is from him. He only is my rock
and my salvation. – Psalm 62:5-6 KJV

It is possible to be waiting continually on God, but not *only* on Him. There may be other secret confidences that intervene and prevent the blessing that was expected. So the word *only* throws light on the path to the fullness and certainty of blessing. *My soul, wait thou only upon God. He only is my rock.*

Yes, *my soul, wait thou only upon God.*

There is only one God and only one source of life and happiness for the heart; *He only is my rock; my soul, wait thou only upon God.* You desire to be good, but *there is none good but one, that is, God,* and there is no possible goodness except what is received directly from Him (Matthew 19:17). You have sought to be holy, but *there is none holy as the LORD,* and there is no holiness except what His Spirit of holiness breathes on us every moment. You would gladly live and work for God and His kingdom, for men and their salvation. He says, *Hast thou not heard that the God of the age is the LORD, the Creator of the ends of the earth? He does not faint, nor is he weary; . . . He gives power to the faint; and to those that have no might he increases strength. . . . those that wait for the LORD shall have new strength* (Isaiah 40:28-31). He only is God; *He only is my rock.*

My soul, wait thou only upon God. You will not find many who can help you in this. Enough brethren will draw you to put trust in churches and doctrines, in schemes and plans and human devices, as a means of grace and divine appointments. But, *my soul, wait thou only upon God* Himself. His most sacred appointments become a snare when we trust in them. The brazen serpent became Nehushtan, an idol; the ark and the temple a vain confidence. Let the living God stand alone with nothing else; let Him be your hope.

My soul, wait thou only upon God. Eyes and hands and feet, mind and thought, may have to be intently engaged in the duties of this life, but *my soul, wait thou only upon God.* You are an immortal spirit, created not for this world but for eternity and for God. O, my soul, realize your destiny. Know your privilege, and *wait thou only upon God.* Don't let interest in religious thoughts and exercises deceive you; they often take the place of waiting upon God. *My soul, wait thou,* thy very self, thy inmost being, with all your power, *wait thou only upon God.* God is for you; you are for God; wait only upon Him.

Yes, *my soul, wait thou only upon God.* Beware of your

two great enemies – the world and self. Beware lest any earthly satisfaction or enjoyment, however innocent it appears, keeps you from saying, *I will enter . . . unto the God of my exceeding joy* (Psalm 43:4). Remember and study what Jesus said about denying self: *Whosoever will come after me, let him deny himself* (Mark 8:34).

Tersteegen, a German religious writer, said, "The saints deny themselves in everything." Pleasing self in little things may be strengthening it to assert itself in greater things. *My soul, wait thou only upon God*; let Him be all thy salvation and all thy desire. Say continually and with an undivided heart, *my expectation is from him*; *He only is my rock*; *I shall not be moved.* Whatever your spiritual or physical need is, whatever the desire or prayer of your heart, whatever your interest is in connection with God's work in the church or the world – in solitude or in the rush of the world, in public worship or other gatherings of the saints – remember: *My soul, wait thou only upon God.* Let your expectations be from Him alone. He only is your Rock.

My soul, wait thou only upon God. Never forget the two foundational truths on which this blessed waiting rests. If you are ever inclined to think this *waiting only* is too hard or too high, "they" will remind you at once. "They" are your absolute helplessness and the absolute sufficiency of your God. Oh, admit the entire sinfulness of all that is of self and don't think of letting self have anything to say. Admit your utter and unceasing inability to ever change what is evil in you or to produce anything that is spiritually good. Enter into deep dependence on God to receive from Him every moment that He gives. Enter into His covenant of redemption with His promise to restore more gloriously than ever what you have lost, and by His Son and Spirit to give within you His actual divine presence and power. Thus, wait upon thy God continually and only.

My soul, wait thou only upon God! No words can tell, no heart conceive, the riches of the glory of this mystery of the Father and of Christ. Our God, in the infinite tenderness and omnipotence of His love, waits to be our life and joy. Oh, my soul, may I no longer need to repeat the words *wait upon God*, but let all that is in me rise and sing: *Truly my soul waiteth upon God* (Psalm 62:1 KJV). *I have waited for thee all the day.*

My soul, wait thou only upon God!

Note

My publishers have issued a work by William Law on the Holy Spirit.[3] In the introduction I wrote for the book, I mentioned how much I owe to Law's book. I believe that anyone who will take the time to read it thoughtfully will find rich spiritual profit in connection with a life of waiting upon God.

What he explains more clearly than I have found anywhere else are these truths:

The very nature and being of God as the only possessor and dispenser of life in the universe imply that He must communicate the power by which it exists to every creature, and therefore the power by which it can do that which is good.

The very nature and being of a creature is due to God alone, and the continuation of that existence is equally due to Him, which implies that the creature's

---

3   William Law, *The Power of the Spirit: A Humble, Earnest, and Affectionate Address to the Clergy*, with additional extracts and introduction by Rev. Andrew Murray, (New York: Fleming H. Revell Company, 1895).

happiness can only be found in absolute, unceasing, moment-by-moment dependence upon God.

The great value and blessing of the gift of the Spirit at Pentecost as the fruit of Christ's redemption is that it is now possible for God to take possession of His redeemed children and work in them, as He did before the fall of Adam. We need to know the restoration of the Holy Spirit as the presence and power of God in us.

In the spiritual life, our great need is the knowledge of two great lessons. The one is our total sinfulness and helplessness, our utter inability by any effort to do anything towards the maintenance and increase of our inner spiritual life. The other is the infinite willingness of God's love, which is nothing but a desire to communicate Himself and His blessedness to us, to meet our every need and every moment work what we need by His Son and Spirit.

Therefore, the very essence of true religion, whether in heaven or upon earth, consists of an unalterable dependence upon God, because we can give God no other glory than yielding ourselves to His love, which created us to show forth its glory that it may now perfect its work in us.

I don't need to point out how deep these truths go to the very root of the spiritual life – especially the life of *waiting upon God*. I am confident that those who are willing to take the time to study this thoughtful writer will appreciate my introduction to his book.

Andrew Murray – A Brief Biography

Andrew Murray had a rich religious ancestry. His grandfather (Andrew) left the occupation of being a shepherd in order to work in the flour mills of Scotland. He was a godly man, and his deathbed prayers influenced his son John to enter the work of the ministry. John became an ordained minister in Scotland. John's younger brother, Andrew, became licensed in the Church of Scotland and was ordained by the Presbytery of Aberdeen. He became a missionary with the Dutch Reformed Church in South Africa.

While in South Africa, Andrew met the woman who would be come his wife – Maria Susanna Stegmann. She was of German ancestry, and her great-grandfather was a Huguenot who had been driven out of France when the Edict of Nantes, which had granted the French Protestants some religious liberty, was revoked. Andrew and Susanna's first son was named John, and their second son, Andrew, is the subject of this brief biography and the author of this book.

Andrew Murray was born in South Africa on May 9, 1828. His father often read stories of revivals to his family. When Andrew was ten years old, he and his brother John were sent to Scotland to be educated. They stayed with their uncle John, the Scottish minister. In 1840, William Burns, the revivalist, spoke in Aberdeen, Scotland. He stayed with their uncle John while there, and Burns' preaching, along with his long, impassioned prayers for revival and the salvation of the lost greatly impacted young Andrew.

Andrew and John went on to attend Marischal College in Aberdeen when Andrew was almost seventeen years old, from which they graduated with the master of arts degree in 1845. From there they studied theology and refreshed themselves in the Dutch language at the University of Utrecht in Holland. Rationalism was popular then. Mr. Murray in South Africa had written to his sons in Holland to be careful of the teaching. In a letter to his sons, dated April 23, 1845, he wrote: "You may soon hear sentiments broached among the students, and even by professors, on theological subjects which may startle you, but be cautious in receiving them, by whatever names or number of names they may be supported. Try to act like the noble Bereans (Acts 17:11). By studying your Bibles and your own hearts I doubt not, under the guidance of the blessed Spirit, you will

be led into all truth. . . . Whatever books may be rec-
ommended to you, be sure not to neglect the study of
the Holy Scriptures. This must be a daily exercise, and
must be attended to with humility and much prayer
for the guidance of the Holy Spirit."

Reminiscent of George Whitefield and the Wesleys
and their Holy Club at Oxford, the Murray brothers
joined a similar group at the University of Utrecht. It
was called *Sechor Dabar* (Remember the Word), and
its purpose was "to promote the study of the subjects
required for the ministerial calling in the spirit of the
Revival." The members of this group were often mocked,
but they desired to live fully for God. On May 9, 1848,
John and Andrew Murray were ordained by the Hague
Committee of the Dutch Reformed Church, and they
returned to South Africa to begin their ministry work.

At the age of twenty-one, Andrew was given the
responsibility of being the only minister in a 50,000
square-mile territory in remote South Africa. For
weeks at a time, Andrew would ride on horseback to
preach to the Dutch-speaking farmers. Andrew married
Emma Rutherford, the daughter of an English pastor,
in 1856. They had eight children together – four boys
and four girls.

In 1860, Andrew Murray accepted the pastorate of
a church in Worcester, South Africa, where they heard
some speakers tell stories of revivals in North American
and Europe. Murray and others prayed earnestly for
revival, and experienced somewhat of a revival, though
not as Murray had expected. He became increasingly

interested in sanctification and what is now commonly called "the holiness movement."

Andrew Murray became the pastor of a church in Cape Town in 1864, and then became a pastor in Wellington in 1877. Also in 1877, Murray traveled to the United States and spent five weeks learning about Sunday schools, Moody's revivals, and the Dutch Reformed Church in America. Murray also attended the Presbyterian Council in Scotland and spoke elsewhere throughout the land, including visits to Holland and Germany.

Murray returned to South Africa where he became increasingly involved in Christian education and in training people for ministry. Murray's speaking schedule over the past few years led to an interesting and influential time in his life. His voice toward the end of 1879 began to be strained, and this difficulty continued for about two years, where he was not often able to speak publicly. He would write out his message at times, and it would be read to the congregation by others. Andrew tried visiting various doctors, traveling to drier climates, and more, but his throat did not improve. He did spend more time studying and writing, though.

After finding only temporary and inadequate improvements, Andrew Murray began studying more about healing by faith. In 1881, Murray was in London. He had wanted to be able to go to Switzerland to visit with a man he had met earlier in life and who was now the head of an institute for faith healing. Murray learned that this man, Otto Stockmaier, was then in London.

They met together and discussed biblical passages related to healing and faith. Stockmaier urged Murray to attend the meetings of an American, Dr. Boardman, who had written on the topic of healing by faith and who then had an institute in London. Murray visited the institute and remained there for three weeks. He was taught that healing by faith was not just to heal the body, but to help one on to holiness and a life of consecration to God.

Murray's voice improved, and he wrote and spoke much on healing by faith after that. He did occasionally have less serious voice trouble later in life at times, and seemed not to place such an emphasis on healing by faith for everyone, but his experience and study certainly caused him to believe in the power and possibility of healing by faith for the rest of his life.

Andrew Murray continued writing and speaking. He was a speaker at the famous annual holiness Keswick conference. He was chosen to be the moderator of his church synod six different times. He wrote over 200 books and pamphlets, many on holiness and the deeper life. His books include *Absolute Surrender, Humility, Abide in Christ, The Deeper Christian Life, The School of Obedience, Waiting on God, The Ministry of Intercession, The New Life, With Christ in the School of Prayer, The Two Covenants and the Second Blessing,* and more.

Andrew Murray spent his last moments on earth praying and rejoicing in the goodness of God. He passed from this life on January 18, 1917, at the age of eighty-eight.

Other Similar Titles